HEARTY

Cast-Iron and Skillet
COOKING

HEARTY
Cast-Iron and Skillet COOKING

101 Easy-to-Make, Feel-Good Recipes

By Anne Schaeffer

FOX CHAPEL
PUBLISHING

ISBN 978-1-4971-0386-3

Recipe selection, design, and book design © Fox Chapel Publishing. Recipes and photographs © G&R Publishing DBA CQ Products, unless otherwise noted.

The following images are credited to Shutterstock.com and their respective creators: page 7: JulieK2; page 9, bottom: Iyly; page 10: E.J. Johnson Photography; page 11, top: BIRYUKOVAEKATERINA; page 11, bottom: VBD Photos; page 63: lentinagar; page 85: A. Zhuravleva; page 89: Marie Sonmez Photography; page 91: Sea Wave; page 94: Africa Studio; page 123: Tatiana Volgutova; page 131: iuliia_n; page 132: Peredniankina; page 136: AnnapolisStudios; page 143: Jim Bowie; page 147: Losangela; page 149: nelea33.

Library of Congress Control Number: 2023936643

To learn more about the other great books from Fox Chapel Publishing, or to find a retailer near you, call toll-free 800-457-9112 or visit us at www.FoxChapelPublishing.com.

We are always looking for talented authors. To submit an idea, please send a brief inquiry to acquisitions@foxchapelpublishing.com.

Printed in China
First printing

Table of Contents

INTRODUCTION

What makes a meal "hearty"? Is it the amount of food on the table? The fullness you feel after you finish eating? Or is it the feeling of comfort when you share a meal with those you love? When I look back on the meals that feel the heartiest, I see that they are the ones shared with my loved ones and cooked on a skillet or cast-iron cookware. There's just something special about meals like this that feel cozy and comforting. The recipes in this book will show you how to make memories through food by turning a normal dish into a hearty, home-cooked meal that you will remember for years to come.

Cast-iron cookware can be used on the stove, in the oven, over a fire, and on the grill.

In this book, you will discover deliciously hearty recipes that can be cooked on the stove, in the oven, and over a fire—all using the same set of cookware. Whether it's a a skillet or a Dutch oven, cast iron can go directly from stovetop to oven and be used with campfires and grills effortlessly, thanks to the handles on both sides, making it easier to lift and move pans. Cast iron is also extremely durable and maintains even cooking temperatures once heated. The food it cooks browns nicely, and crusts are always crisp. And its nonstick surface is natural, with no artificial chemical coatings in sight—just the natural oils you use to season the cookware. A bit of iron even transfers to the food, bumping up the iron content for your body to absorb. But my favorite part of cooking with cast iron is that this cookware will last for generations, which means you won't be shopping for new skillets or Dutch ovens anytime soon. So, not only will this cookware be passed down through your family for years to come, but so will the delicious recipes and memories that you create with them. When you discover cast iron, you discover the tradition of comfort food.

What if you don't have cast-iron skillets, but still want that rustic, comforting taste? Any skillet on or inside the stove will do just fine. All the skillet recipes in this book will work perfectly with a normal iron skillet. What truly makes a meal hearty isn't necessarily the type of cookware or appliance you use—although that helps—but the people you share it with. So, let's get our campfires and ovens started and get cooking.

Anne Schaeffer

CAST-IRON COOKING

Skillets are easily transferable from stovetop to oven—just remember to use potholders, since the handles can get hot.

An enamel indoor-only kitchen-style Dutch oven should only be used on a stovetop or in the oven.

Use a camp-style Dutch oven outdoors, either over hot coals, a flame, or on the grill.

In this book, we'll be using two types of cast-iron cookware: skillets and Dutch ovens. If you want to take the Dutch oven out to the campfire, you'll want to grab a camp-style oven. Let's take a look at the basics of each before we get started.

Skillets

Cast-iron skillets can be used indoors on a stovetop, in an oven, and even outdoors on a grate over a fire, hot coals, or propane burner. If yours doesn't have a lid, be sure to have foil on hand for covering so you can trap all the heat and delicious flavors inside.

Dutch Ovens

We'll use two types of Dutch ovens: kitchen style and camp style. If you have an indoor-only, kitchen-style oven with enamel coating, a flat bottom without legs, and a wire bail, be careful to only use this on the stove or in the oven. If you want to venture outside, you can use a kitchen-style Dutch oven without enamel coating, a flat bottom without legs, and a wire bail (a handle meant to hang the pot over the fire). This can be used on the stove, in the oven (use caution on glass-top stoves), as well as outdoors on a grate, or hanging from a tripod over a fire or hot coals.

A camp-style Dutch oven without enamel coating, a flat bottom with legs, and a wire bail is best used outdoors with a fire or hot coals. You can use it indoors too, but only inside the oven: set the pot on a baking sheet on the lowest rack.

TAKE CARE

Cast-iron cookware are made to last, but there are some steps you can make to ensure that they're properly cared for. By seasoning and cleaning your cast-iron skillet or Dutch oven, you'll not only be preserving the cookware, but also enhancing the flavor of your food.

Seasoning

Seasoning is vital to not only coating the cookware to prevent rust, but also to creating a natural, permanent nonstick cooking surface. Simply rub a thin layer of vegetable oil or shortening over all surfaces and set the pan upside down on a rack in a 350°F oven for 1 hour (put foil on the bottom of the oven to catch drips). Turn off the oven and let the pan cool completely; wipe with a paper towel. Refresh as needed and cook periodically with oil to build patina.

Seasoning is a must in cast-iron cooking. Use vegetable oil or shortening for best results.

Cleaning

With water: Use very hot water and a stiff nylon brush or scrubber. Rinse and wipe dry with paper towels or an old towel (cast iron can leave black stains). Then set on a burner over low heat to remove any remaining moisture and prevent rust.

Without water: Scrub with coarse salt or a plastic scraper and wipe with a clean rag.

It's best to avoid using dish soap, since it strips off the seasoning, but if you feel it's necessary, use it sparingly and remember to refresh the seasoning on your cookware afterwards.

You can clean cast iron with or without water to preserve the seasoning of the cookware.

Storing

After all the moisture has been removed and the cast-iron is cool, store it uncovered in a dry location. Remember not to reseason your cookware before you store it, or the oil could turn rancid before you use it again. If rust appears, scrub it off with steel wool and reseason.

Store your cleaned and dry cast-iron cookware in a dry location.

Building the Perfect Cooking Fire

First things first: you'll only get a nice cooking fire if you use the right kind of firewood. Use split logs since they produce the best heat and are easiest to ignite. Hard woods such as maple, walnut, oak, or apple are best; they burn slowly and produce wonderful cooking coals.

Pile up tinder in the cooking area; light it with a match or lighter. When the tinder is burning well, place kindling loosely on top, adding more as needed. Once the kindling is burning nicely, carefully add split firewood, teepee-style, over the burning kindling. When the flames die down, white hot coals remain. Use a metal fire poker or long stick to distribute the coals for cooking, as needed.

Building a stable fire for cooking is only the first step of making a delicious cast-iron meal.

CAMPFIRE SAFETY TIPS AND TRICKS

- Make sure it is legal to build a fire in your location.
- Use a fire pit, if available. Otherwise, build your fire on rock or dirt and construct a U-shaped perimeter with large rocks.
- Build your fire at least 8 feet away from flammable objects.
- Never use gas or kerosene on a fire, as they pose a serious risk of explosion.
- Never leave a fire unattended.
- Don't build a fire if it's windy. Sparks can cause unintended fires.
- Protect hands with leather gloves or heavy oven mitts and use long tongs to prevent burns.
- Fill a bucket with water and keep it near the fire to douse flare-ups.
- Extinguish your fire when you're finished using it by dousing it with plenty of water. Be sure all the coals, embers, and wood are wet and cool.
- If you don't have access to water, smother the fire with sand or dirt to extinguish it. You should still be sure all the coals, embers, and wood are completely cool.

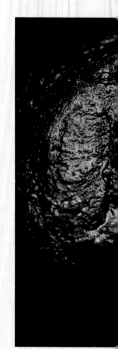

Determining Heat

Some of the recipes in this book recommend cooking over a fire that is a certain heat level or temperature. You can use the following method to judge the temperature of your campfire. Hold your hand about 4 inches over the coals. Count the number of seconds you can hold your hand in place before it gets too hot to keep it there.

Some things you should know:

Every skillet has a maximum "safe" temperature, that is, the highest temperature it can tolerate. Certain cookware can survive even the hottest temperatures, some are safe only to low oven temperatures, and others aren't oven-safe at all. Be sure you know how resilient yours is before using it for a recipe for the oven.

For some recipes, the size of the skillet won't matter, but for others, the cooking or baking times might need to be adjusted if you use a skillet other than what's called for in a recipe. As a rule of thumb, an 8" or 9" skillet is great for one or two people, and a 9" or 10" one works well for two to four.

Determining the correct heat of your fire is crucial to cooking your dishes to perfection.

CAMPFIRE COOKING TEMPERATURES

How long can you hold your hand 4" over the coals?

2 seconds = about 500°F (High heat)

3 seconds = about 400°F (Medium-High heat)

4 seconds = about 350°F (Medium heat)

5 seconds = about 300°F (Low heat)

Food Temperature Safety

No matter the heat of your fire, always make sure your food is thoroughly cooked. Ground meat, chicken, and pork should be cooked until it is no longer pink and juices run clear. But color isn't a foolproof guide. It is best to use a good meat thermometer to prevent under- or over-cooking. The USDA recommends the following minimum internal temperatures:

- Fish: 145°F
- Beef Roasts: 145°F (rare) to 160°F (medium) to 170°F (well done)
- Ground Beef: 160°F
- Ground Poultry: 165°F
- Chicken Breasts: 170°F
- Whole Poultry and Parts (thighs, wings): 180°F
- Pork (chops, tenderloins): 160°F
- Ground Pork: 160°F
- Egg Dishes: 160°F
- Reheating Foods: 165°F or until hot and steaming

Properly take the temperature of any meats you cook to ensure the safety of your guests.

CAMPFIRE COOKING TIPS

For outdoor cast-iron Dutch oven cooking, using a charcoal chimney starter is a quick and easy way to get coals hot. Fill the top portion with unlit coals, push crumpled newspaper into the bottom portion, and light the newspapers from the bottom.

When the coals are hot, start cooking using the number of coals suggested in the recipe. If the food needs to cook for more than 30 to 45 minutes, have extra hot coals ready so cooking can continue without interruption.

The temperature inside the pot depends on the number and placement of hot coals or the distance of the pot from the heat. Sometimes you spread hot coals in a flat layer underneath the pot to give it plenty of heat for boiling, browning, or frying. To bake, simmer, or roast foods, you'll need heat from both the bottom and top, so arrange some hot coals in a ring underneath the pot and place more hot coals on the lid.

Step 1: Fill the chimney with coals and light from the bottom.

Step 2: Cook the number of coals that you need for the recipe.

Step 3: Spread the coals evenly.

FOLLOWING THE RECIPES	
If it says...	It means...
24+ hot coals	Start with 24 hot charcoal briquettes, but light extras to complete the cooking.
About 24 hot coals	Use about 24 hot charcoal briquettes to complete the cooking.
Cook on a grate	Start with the grate 3" to 4" above heat and adjust it up or down as needed for correct cooking temperature.
Medium heat	Use medium setting on a gas grill, or judge by holding your palm above the fire for 4 seconds at about the position the food will cook (2 seconds = hot heat; 5 seconds = low heat).

COOKING WITH VARIOUS DUTCH OVEN SIZES

Diameter	Volume	Uses
5"	1 pint	Melt butter, make basting sauce, make individual desserts
6"	1 quart	Prepare small portions of recipes or sauces
8"	2 quarts	Prepare sauces, toppings or vegetables, warm leftovers
10"	4 quarts	Prepare a complete meal for two; prepare soups, cornbread, main dishes or side dishes
10"	5 quarts	Prepare main or side dishes
12"	6 quarts	Prepare main or side dishes
12"	8 quarts	Prepare whole chicken or roast, bread, or standing rib roast; prepare main or side dishes
14"	8 quarts	Prepare meals for larger groups, such as a roast with vegetables, large stews, or cobblers
14"	10 quarts	Roast a small turkey or ham, bake a large batch of bread, prepare large meals or side dishes
16"	12 quarts	Use to double any recipes calling for a 12" oven, prepare large meals or side dishes

Rotate the pot and lid every 10 to 15 minutes to prevent hot spots. Just lift the pot and rotate it clockwise one-third turn, and rotate the lid one-third turn in the opposite direction. Check your food often. Coals get very hot but tend to burn out and lose heat after 30 to 45 minutes. You may need to add fresh hot coals to maintain the correct temperature.

Stacked cooking can be used to cook foods in two Dutch ovens using shared coals. Just set one Dutch oven on top of another, with coals from the lid of the bottom Dutch oven creating heat under the pot on top. If you're

Step 4: Placing coals on top of the lid promotes an even heat distribution.

Step 5: When cooking more than one dish at a time, or when cooking sides or sauces, you can stack your Dutch ovens on top of each other.

BREAKFAST

The flavors of a hearty breakfast—salty meats, rich dough, fresh fruits and vegetables—only become more enhanced when cooking with cast iron. These breakfast recipes will help you start your day with a fulfilling, delicious meal to give you energy for whatever lies ahead.

Bacon & Potato Pancakes

SERVES 2

Ingredients

- **1½ pounds yellow potatoes, peeled and diced**
- **4 bacon strips**
- **½ (13.5 ounce) can coconut milk**
- **2 eggs**
- **2 teaspoons chives, chopped**
- **¾ teaspoon salt**
- **Maple syrup, sour cream, bacon, or chives, for serving**

On the Stove

12"

1. Cook potatoes in boiling water in a big nonstick skillet until soft; drain and dump into a bowl.

2. Dry the skillet and cook bacon until crisp; chop and set aside.

3. Add coconut milk to the potatoes; mash until combined. Beat in 2 eggs until incorporated. Beat in more coconut milk, until the consistency of pancake batter.

4. Stir in chives, the set-aside bacon, and salt.

5. Wipe out most of the grease from the skillet; heat on medium heat. For each pancake, slowly pour ⅓ cup batter into the skillet and cook to brown both sides, turning once.

6. Serve with maple syrup, sour cream, bacon, and/or chives.

Carrot Cake Pancakes

Ingredients

- 1 teaspoon baking powder
- ¼ teaspoon salt
- Flour, as needed
- ½ teaspoon ground allspice
- 2½ tablespoons sugar
- 2 eggs
- ¾ cup shredded carrots
- ½ cup milk
- ½ cup plain yogurt, plus more for serving
- ⅓ cup golden raisins
- Vegetable oil, as needed
- Honey or maple syrup, for serving

Over the Fire

1. Put the baking powder and salt in a ¾-cup measuring cup; fill with flour and dump into a bowl (you can replace these three ingredients with 1 cup self-rising flour).

2. Add the allspice, sugar, eggs, carrots, milk, and ½ cup yogurt. Grab a spoon and stir to combine, then stir in the raisins.

3. Heat a griddle or skillet on a rack over a medium cooking fire (not too hot–you want these pancakes to cook all the way through without burning) and add a little oil.

4. Use a ½-cup measuring cup to pour batter into the hot oil and to spread the batter out slightly. Flip the pancakes once the bottoms are golden brown, then cook until the other sides are golden.

5. Serve with honey or syrup and a dollop of yogurt.

Ingredients

- **2 eggs**
- **1 red onion**
- **1 jalapeño pepper**
- **¼ cup butter**
- **Salt and pepper, to taste**
- **8 ounces firm goat cheese, crumbled**
- **2 tablespoons fresh chives, finely chopped**
- **Toast, muffins, or pastries, optional**

SERVES 2

Zippy Scrambled Eggs

Preparation

In a medium bowl, lightly beat eggs and set aside. Finely chop onion to measure ¾ cup. Slice jalapeño into thin rounds, keeping seeds as desired.

On the Stove or over the Fire (24 hot coals)

12"

1. Place skillet on stovetop or grate over medium-high heat and melt butter. Add onion and jalapeño; sauté until tender.

2. Stir in eggs and season with salt and pepper. Continue to cook and stir until soft curds form or to desired doneness.

3. Remove skillet from heat and stir in cheese and chives.

4. Serve promptly with toast, muffins, or pastries as desired.

Swiss Vegetable Omelet

SERVES 1

Ingredients

- **1 tablespoon butter**
- **¼ cup onion, chopped**
- **½ cup asparagus, sliced**
- **¼ cup zucchini, sliced and halved**
- **¼ cup red bell pepper, chopped**
- **2 mushrooms, sliced**
- **Salt and pepper, to taste**
- **4 eggs**
- **2 tablespoons milk**
- **¼ cup shredded Swiss cheese**

On the Stove or over the Fire

10"

1. Melt butter in a 10-inch skillet over medium heat.

2. Add onion, asparagus, zucchini, red bell pepper, and mushrooms; sauté until just tender, stirring occasionally. Transfer veggies to a bowl; season with salt.

3. In a separate bowl, beat eggs, milk, and salt and black pepper.

4. Melt enough butter in the skillet to coat the bottom. Add the eggs and cook over medium-low heat 3 to 4 minutes, until the bottom begins to set.

5. Lift the edges to let the uncooked portion flow toward the outside. Cook until the center starts to look dry.

6. Top with Swiss cheese and the veggies. Gently fold omelet in half and cook until the cheese melts.

Simple Dutch Oven Omelet

Ingredients

- **10 large eggs**
- **2 cups milk**
- **1 cup grated Parmesan cheese**
- **1 cup diced cooked ham**
- **¼ cup fresh flat-leaf parsley, finely chopped**
- **1 teaspoon salt**
- **Freshly ground black pepper, to taste**

Preparation

Beat the eggs in a large bowl and whisk in the milk. Stir in the cheese, diced ham, and parsley. Season with the salt and pepper.

On the Stove and in the Oven

1. Preheat oven to 375°F. Meanwhile, place Dutch oven on stovetop over medium heat.

2. Lightly grease the oven with olive oil if you like. When hot, pour egg mixture into Dutch oven.

3. Transfer to center rack in oven to bake uncovered for 45 minutes or until the top is slightly golden and a knife inserted in the middle comes out clean.

4. Let cool for 5 minutes before slicing. Serve hot.

Over the Fire or on the Grill (28 hot coals)

1. Preheat and oil Dutch oven to 375°F using 11 coals under the oven and 17 coals on the lid. This will brown the top of the omelet.

2. When hot, pour egg mixture into the Dutch oven. Bake for 45 minutes or until the top is slightly golden and a knife inserted in the middle comes out clean.

3. When you see steam coming out from under the lid, you know it is done. Let cool for 5 minutes before slicing. Serve hot.

Thick & Chewy A.M. Pizza

Ingredients

- ½ pound applewood-smoked bacon strips
- ½ red onion, diced
- ½ pound ground breakfast sausage
- 1 pound frozen pizza dough, thawed
- 1 cup shredded Colby cheese
- 1 cup shredded provolone cheese
- 4 eggs
- 2 tablespoons water
- Onion powder, garlic salt, and black pepper, to taste
- Grated Parmesan cheese

On the Stove and in the Oven

1. Cook the bacon in the pot of a 10-inch, kitchen-style Dutch oven until crisp; drain on paper towels, and pour the grease out of the pot. Crumble the bacon into a big bowl.

2. Return the pot to the heat and cook the onion and sausage until browned, crumbling it as it cooks. Pour the mixture into the bowl with the bacon and set aside. Let the pot cool, then line with foil and grease lightly.

3. Press the dough over the bottom and 1 inch up the side.

4. Partially bake the crust in a preheated 350°F oven for 5 minutes.

5. Press the set-aside meat mixture into the crust and sprinkle with the Colby and provolone cheeses.

6. In a bowl, whisk together the eggs, water, and seasoning; pour slowly and evenly over the crust so it seeps in but doesn't overflow. Sprinkle with Parmesan cheese.

7. Bake in a 350°F oven for 20 minutes, until the crust is golden and the eggs are set.

8. Let pizza stand 5 minutes, then remove from the pot by lifting the foil. Slice and serve.

Over the Fire (20 hot coals)

1. Using a camp-style Dutch oven instead, follow steps 1–3 above.

2. Cover with the lid and set on a ring of 7 hot coals. Partially bake the crust for 5 to 8 minutes.

3. Follow steps 5–6 above.

4. Cover the pot and put 12 more hot coals scattered on the lid. Bake 20 to 25 minutes, until crust is golden, and the eggs are set, rotating the pot and lid several times and moving coals as needed.

5. Let pizza stand 5 minutes, then remove from the pot by lifting the foil. Slice and serve.

Cheesy Bacon Pull-Aparts

Ingredients

- 2 (16.3 ounce) tubes large flaky layers refrigerated biscuits
- ⅔ cup vegetable-flavored cream cheese spread (try garden vegetable, chive, or spicy jalapeño)
- ½ cup bacon bits or crumbled cooked bacon
- 4 green onions, finely chopped
- 8 deli slices cheddar, American, or Swiss cheese, quartered
- Sour Cream & Onion Dip (see recipe on page 25)

Preparation

1. Grease a 9-inch, square aluminum baking pan and set inside a second one. Separate each biscuit into two layers.

2. Spread 1 teaspoon cream cheese on each layer and top with 1 to 2 teaspoons bacon bits, ½ teaspoon green onion, and ¼ slice of cheese. Stack eight layers on top of each other, repeating to make four stacks.

3. Set one stack on its side along the side of the pan, starting in one corner (make sure the side without filling touches the edge of the pan). Set a second stack in the pan at a right angle to the first stack. Set the remaining two stacks around the edges to fill the pan.

In the Oven

1. Set the pan on risers (balls of foil or several canning jar rings for instance) in the pot of a big kitchen-style Dutch oven and cover with the lid.

2. Bake in a 350°F oven about an hour or until puffy, brown, and no longer doughy. Dunk bites of bread into dip if desired.

Over the Fire (About 12 hot coals)

1. Set the pan on risers in the pot of a big camp-style Dutch oven. Cover and set on a ring of 12 hot coals with a few more hot coals on the lid.

2. Bake 50 to 60 minutes, until puffy, brown, and no longer doughy. Rotate the pot and lid every 15 minutes and check for doneness several times, replenishing or removing coals as needed. Dunk bites of bread into dip if desired.

SOUR CREAM & ONION DIP

- ⅓ cup canola oil
- ½ cup onion, finely chopped
- salt
- ¼ teaspoon sugar
- 1 cup sour cream

Heat oil in a small skillet. When hot, add onion, a pinch of salt, and sugar; cook until browned. Drain off the oil and stir onion into sour cream. Makes 1 cup.

Egg, Ham & Cheese Quesadilla

SERVES 1

Ingredients

- 1 teaspoon butter
- ¾ cup diced ham
- ¼ red bell pepper, diced
- Black olives, sliced
- 4 eggs, beaten
- Salt, pepper, and dry mustard, to taste
- 2 (10-inch) flour tortillas
- 4 to 5 slices mozzarella cheese
- 4 to 5 slices cheddar cheese

On the Stove or over the Fire

12"

1. Melt butter in a 12-inch skillet over medium heat. Add ham, red bell pepper, and black olives; sauté until the peppers are slightly softened, stirring often.

2. Add eggs and season with salt, black pepper, and dry mustard; cook and stir until the eggs are scrambled and set. Transfer everything to a bowl.

3. Wipe out the skillet and place a tortilla in it. Layer on mozzarella cheese, the egg mixture, and cheddar cheese. Top with a second tortilla.

4. Cover and heat over medium-low heat until golden on the bottom and the cheese starts to melt; flip carefully and heat until the other side is golden. Slice and share.

Hearty Breakfast Skillet

SERVES 2

Ingredients

- ½ pound tiny potatoes
- Chicken broth
- Butter, as needed
- 3 eggs
- 2 teaspoons water

- ½ cup shredded cheddar cheese
- Prosciutto, chopped
- Red bell pepper, chopped
- Green onion, chopped
- Sour cream, for topping

On the Stove and in the Oven

9"

1. Place tiny potatoes in a single layer in a 9-inch, oven-safe skillet; add chicken broth to cover them halfway. Bring to a boil; cover and cook over medium heat for 5 minutes.

2. Uncover and cook 5 minutes longer. Toss several pats of butter over the potatoes. Cook without stirring until liquid evaporates.

3. Flatten slightly and cook until the bottoms are brown.

4. Preheat your oven to 400°F. Beat eggs with water and pour over the potatoes. Reduce heat to medium-low, cover, and cook until the eggs begin to set.

5. Transfer the skillet to the oven to finish cooking. Sprinkle with shredded cheddar cheese. Once melted, add prosciutto, red bell pepper, green onion, and sour cream.

Sweet Potato Skillet

SERVES 2

Ingredients

- 1 tablespoon vegetable oil
- 1 large sweet potato, peeled and diced
- 1 Anaheim pepper, chopped
- Onion salt and black pepper, to taste
- Spinach or kale, chopped, as needed
- Minced garlic, to taste
- 2 eggs

On the Stove

12"

1. Heat vegetable oil in a big skillet over medium heat.
2. Put sweet potato and Anaheim pepper into the hot oil and sprinkle with onion salt and black pepper.
3. Cook until the veggies are slightly soft, stirring occasionally. Push the veggies to one side of the skillet; toss a couple of big handfuls of spinach or kale and garlic into the empty space.
4. When the greens begin to wilt, push those to the side and crack the eggs into the empty space. Cook until done the way you like them and season as you wish.

Over the Fire

Cook on a grate over hot coals instead and follow all steps above.

Sweet Potato Frittata

SERVES 6

Ingredients

- 2 tablespoons olive oil
- 2 cups sweet potatoes, peeled and diced
- 1 cup onion, sliced
- Salt and black pepper, to taste
- 1 cup diced cooked ham
- 8 eggs
- ⅓ cup shredded sharp cheddar cheese
- 1 teaspoon dried rosemary
- ¼ cup crumbled feta cheese

In the Oven

1. Heat olive oil in the pot of a 10-inch kitchen-style Dutch oven.

2. Add sweet potatoes and onion; season with salt and black pepper. After a few minutes, add ham; cook until the vegetables are just tender, stirring often.

3. Drain the oil from the pot. In a bowl, whisk together eggs, sharp cheddar cheese, dried rosemary, and salt and pepper; pour gently over the vegetables and top with feta cheese.

4. Bake uncovered in a 350°F oven for 16 to 18 minutes, until the eggs are set. Slice and serve.

On the Grill

(21 hot coals)

1. Using a 10-inch camp-style Dutch oven on a rack over coals instead, follow steps 1–3 above.

2. Cover the pot and set on a ring of 9 hot coals with 12 hot coals on the lid.

3. Cook until the eggs are nearly set, checking every 10 minutes, and rotating the pot and lid.

4. Remove from the heat and let stand to finish cooking. Slice and serve.

Greens & Things Frittata

Ingredients

- **8 strips bacon, diced**
- **4 green onions, sliced**
- **¾ pound asparagus, sliced**
- **6 baby portobello mushrooms, sliced**
- **10 eggs, beaten**
- **1 cup shredded Swiss cheese, divided**
- **½ teaspoon garlic pepper**
- **½ teaspoon dried tarragon**
- **Salt, to taste**
- **Handful of cherry tomatoes, halved**

On the Stove and in the Oven

1. In the pot of a 10-inch kitchen-style Dutch oven, cook the bacon until crisp; drain and set aside.

2. Remove most of the grease from the pot and add the green onions and asparagus; cook until the asparagus is bright green. Add the mushrooms and cook briefly.

3. Add the eggs and ¾ cup of the Swiss cheese; season with garlic pepper, tarragon, and salt. Sprinkle the set-aside bacon, the cherry tomatoes, and the remaining ¼ cup Swiss cheese over the top.

4. Bake uncovered in a 350°F oven for 20 to 25 minutes or until the eggs are set. Slice and serve.

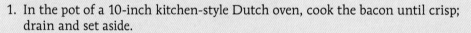

Over the Fire (24 hot coals)

1. Using a camp-style Dutch oven instead, follow steps 1–3 above. Set the pot on a ring of 9 hot coals with 15 hot coals on the lid.

2. Cook until the eggs are nearly done, checking every 10 minutes, rotating the pot and lid. Remove from the heat and let stand covered to finish cooking. Slice and serve.

GREEN GREEK FRITTATA

Use these ingredients instead for a Greek variation, following directions on page 30:

- **8 strips bacon (diced)**
- **1 pound baby spinach (wilted and squeezed dry)**
- **6 sliced baby Portobello mushrooms**
- **10 eggs, beaten**
- **½ cup crumbled feta cheese**
- **¼ cup each chopped chives and parsley**
- **½ teaspoon coriander**
- **Salt and black pepper, to taste**
- **Cherry tomatoes, for garnish**

Cook bacon and baby spinach, reserving some of the cooked bacon for garnish. Add mushrooms and cook briefly. Add eggs, cheese, chives, parsley, coriander, salt, and pepper. Sprinkle with cooked bacon and some halved cherry tomatoes.

Southwest Hash

Ingredients

- 3 tablespoons olive oil
- 2 cups diced turnips or potatoes
- 1½ tablespoons taco seasoning
- 1 teaspoon salt
- ½ onion, diced
- 1 bell pepper, any color, diced
- 1 teaspoon minced garlic
- 4 eggs
- Toppings such as shredded Mexican cheese, salsa, cilantro, and/or lime wedges

On the Stove

1. Heat the oil in a big skillet over medium-high heat. Add the turnips, taco seasoning, and salt and cook about 5 minutes, stirring occasionally.

2. Add the onion, bell pepper, and garlic and cook 3 minutes more, until the vegetables begin to soften.

3. Make four divots in the hash and crack an egg in each. Cover and cook a few minutes more, until the egg whites are set.

4. Serve and add desired toppings.

Over the Fire

Use a grate over a campfire instead, and follow all steps above.

Ingredients

- **3 tablespoons olive oil**
- **1 (14 ounce) package turkey kielbasa, sliced into ¼-inch rounds**
- **1 green bell pepper, diced**
- **½ red bell pepper, diced**
- **1 small sweet onion, diced**
- **Salt and black pepper, to taste**
- **2 large Yukon gold potatoes**
- **Canola oil**

SERVES 4

Skillet Kielbasa Hash

12"

On the Stove and Over the Fire

1. Heat 1 tablespoon oil in a skillet; add the kielbasa and fry for 5 minutes, shaking the skillet a time or two to brown evenly.

2. Transfer the kielbasa to a paper-towel-lined plate to drain. Add the diced veggies to the skillet, season with salt and pepper, and cook until crisp-tender, stirring occasionally.

3. Transfer to the plate with the kielbasa and let everything cool. Put the kielbasa and veggies together in a covered container and chill.

4. Dice the potatoes. In a heavy skillet over a fire or on a grill, heat 2 tablespoons oil over medium-high heat.

5. Add the potatoes and season with salt and pepper. Fry until golden brown, stirring a few times to brown evenly.

6. Add the chilled kielbasa and veggie mixture, toss to combine, and heat through. Serve.

Brussels Hash

SERVES 4

10"

Ingredients

- **½ pound pork sausage**
- **1 tablespoon vegetable oil**
- **1 onion, diced**
- **1 sweet potato, peeled and diced**
- **½ teaspoon minced garlic**
- **½ pound Bussels sprouts**
- **Salt and black pepper, to taste**
- **4 eggs**

On the Stove

1. Fry sausage in hot oil in a medium skillet over medium heat until done, crumbling it with a wooden spoon while it cooks.

2. Add onion and sweet potato; sauté 5 to 7 minutes, until crisp-tender, stirring occasionally.

3. Stir in garlic and cook for 1 minute.

4. Trim and slice brussels sprouts and add to the pan; sauté about 5 minutes, until tender, stirring often. Cook without stirring for 5 minutes, until the bottom starts to brown. Stir in salt and black pepper to taste.

5. Create four small wells in the hash and crack an egg into each. Cover and cook until the eggs are done the way you like them.

6. Season again with salt and pepper and serve.

Biscuits & Gravy

SERVES
4

Ingredients

- ½ pound ground pork sausage
- 2 tablespoons flour
- 2 cups milk
- Salt and pepper, to taste
- ½ cup butter
- 8 refrigerator buttermilk biscuits

On the Stove and in the Oven

9"

1. Cook pork sausage in a small skillet over medium heat until done, crumbling it while it cooks; whisk in flour.

2. Gradually stir in milk, cooking and stirring until thickened. Season with salt and pepper; keep warm.

3. In another small skillet, melt butter. Set biscuits in the butter and turn to coat both sides; sprinkle with salt.

4. Bake in a 375°F oven until the biscuits are done.

5. Serve warm gravy over biscuits.

Over the Fire

9"

1. Using a grate over a campfire instead, follow steps 1–3 above.

2. Cover the skillet and set on a rack over hot embers until the biscuits are brown on both sides and no longer doughy, flipping once.

3. Serve warm gravy over biscuits.

LUNCH

The recipes in this section range from light mid-day snacks to hearty lunch dishes that will leave you wanting more. Some of these recipes may also work well as a side dish for a dinner recipe. Feel free to mix and match!

Sausage & Kraut Skillet

SERVES 4

Ingredients

- ½ pound kielbasa
- 1 tablespoon butter
- ½ medium onion, chopped
- ½ apple, peeled, cored, and shredded
- 1 tablespoon brown sugar
- ¼ teaspoon caraway seed
- ½ small green bell pepper, chopped
- 4 small red potatoes
- ¾ cup drained sauerkraut
- Salt and black pepper, to taste

On the Stove

1. Cut kielbasa or apple-flavored sausage into chunks and set aside.

2. Melt butter in a medium skillet over medium heat. Add onion and cook until tender.

3. Stir in apple, brown sugar, caraway seed, green bell pepper, potatoes, and sauerkraut. Arrange the set-aside sausage on top; cover and cook on medium-low heat for 30 minutes, until the potatoes are tender.

4. Season with salt and black pepper to taste.

12"

Beef Fried Rice

SERVES 2

Ingredients

- 2 tablespoons canola oil, divided
- 2 egg yolks
- ½ red bell pepper
- 1 cup broccoli florets
- ½ (14 ounce) can bean sprouts, drained (about 1 cup)
- 1 cup leftover cooked roast beef, cubed
- 2 cups cooked rice
- 3 tablespoons soy sauce
- Black pepper, to taste
- ¼ cup orange marmalade
- 1 green onion, thinly sliced

On the Stove

10"

1. In a skillet over medium heat, heat 1 tablespoon of the oil.

2. In a bowl, whisk the egg yolks and add them to the hot skillet. Cook until set, transfer to a plate, and mash with a fork.

3. Return the skillet to high heat, place the bell pepper half in the hot skillet until lightly charred on both sides, turning once; cut into bite-size pieces. Set all aside.

4. Return the skillet to high heat and add the remaining 1 tablespoon oil. Add the broccoli and sprouts and sauté a minute or so, until just hot, stirring constantly.

5. Stir in the roast beef, rice, soy sauce, and set-aside roasted peppers; season with black pepper and stir in the marmalade and set-aside egg.

6. Cook until heated through and the broccoli is crisp-tender, tossing constantly. Serve topped with sliced green onion.

Ingredients

- **1 tablespoon olive oil**
- **½ pound ground turkey**
- **Coarse salt and black pepper, to taste**
- **½ teaspoon minced garlic**
- **½ cup diced red bell pepper**
- **¼ cup diced onion**
- **2 tablespoons hoisin sauce**
- **1 tablespoon soy sauce**
- **¼ teaspoon grated fresh gingerroot**
- **½ cup ready rice (I used multigrain medley) or leftover cooked rice**
- **1 green onion, thinly sliced**
- **Lettuce leaves, as needed**
- **Sliced almonds, for garnish**

Asian Turkey Lettuce Wraps

SERVES 2

On the Stove

1. Heat the oil in a medium skillet over medium-high heat.

2. Add the ground turkey and fry until browned, crumbling it while it cooks; transfer to paper towels and season with salt and black pepper.

3. Toss the garlic, bell pepper, and onion into the skillet and sauté 3 to 4 minutes or until tender, stirring often; drain the excess grease.

4. Add the hoisin sauce, soy sauce, gingerroot, and drained turkey, stirring until well blended. Then add the rice and green onion, tossing gently to combine.

5. Put several spoonfuls of the mixture in the center of lettuce leaves and sprinkle with almonds; roll up and secure with picks. Serve and enjoy.

Pesto Flatbread Quesadilla

SERVES 2

Ingredients

- **2 flatbreads**
- **1 roasted garlic bulb**
- **2 teaspoons olive oil**
- **1½ tablespoons pesto**
- **1½ cups shredded rotisserie chicken**
- **1 tomato, chopped**
- **¾ cup shredded Italian cheese blend**

On the Stove

1. To roast the garlic, discard papery outer layers of a whole garlic bulb. Cut off ¼ inch to ½ inch of the top, exposing the individual cloves. Set upright in a muffin pan, drizzle with olive oil, cover with foil, and bake at 400°F for 30 minutes. Squeeze cloves out of their skins and mash.

2. Place 2 flatbreads on a work surface. On half of each, spread half of roasted garlic bulb followed by pesto.

3. Divide shredded rotisserie chicken, tomato, and Italian cheese blend over the pesto; fold flatbreads in half to cover the filling.

4. Preheat a big skillet over medium heat and spritz with cooking spray. Brown the flatbread in the hot skillet, turning once. Serve and enjoy.

12"

Ingredients

- **1 cup uncooked elbow macaroni**
- **2 teaspoons vegetable oil**
- **½ small shallot, chopped**
- **½ teaspoon minced garlic**
- **¼ pound Brussels sprouts, trimmed and sliced**
- **1 tablespoon butter**
- **1 tablespoon flour**
- **¾ cup milk**
- **3 tablespoons half and half**
- **¾ cup shredded fontina cheese**
- **½ cup shredded white cheddar cheese**
- **1½ tablespoons grated Parmesan cheese**
- **Pinch of ground nutmeg**
- **3 fully cooked bacon strips, chopped**
- **1 tablespoon dry breadcrumbs**
- **2 tablespoons panko breadcrumbs**

SERVES 4

3-Cheese Mac with Brussels Sprouts

9"

On the Stove and in the Oven

1. Preheat your oven to 375°F.

2. Cook the macaroni in a 9-inch oven-safe skillet to al dente according to package directions; drain and set aside. Dry out the skillet.

3. Heat the oil in the same skillet over medium-low heat; add the shallot, garlic, and Brussels sprouts. Sauté for 5 minutes, until softened, stirring often; add to the cooked macaroni.

4. Melt the butter in the empty skillet. Whisk in the flour and cook a minute or so, until golden brown. Whisk in the milk and half and half; cook over medium heat until slightly thickened, stirring constantly.

5. Add the fontina, cheddar, Parmesan, and nutmeg, stirring until the cheese is melted.

6. Dump the macaroni, sprouts, and one-third of the bacon into the skillet and stir until well combined. Sprinkle both kinds of breadcrumbs over the top and toss on the remaining bacon.

7. Bake uncovered 30 to 35 minutes or until golden brown and bubbly.

Creamy Mac & Cheese

SERVES 6

Ingredients

- **3 cups milk**
- **2 ½ cups water**
- **Salt, to taste**
- **1 (16 ounce) package uncooked elbow macaroni**
- **2 tablespoons unsalted butter**
- **1 teaspoon Dijon mustard**
- **1 (12 ounce) can evaporated milk**
- **1 teaspoon paprika or smoked paprika**
- **2 cups shredded cheddar cheese, room temperature**
- **Cooked bacon, roasted red bell peppers, and/or chives, for topping**

On the Stove  12"

1. In the pot of a kitchen-style Dutch oven, combine the milk, water, and a little salt. Bring to a boil, stirring often; stir in the macaroni. Cook for 8 to 10 minutes, until al dente; do not drain.

2. Reduce heat, add the butter, mustard, evaporated milk, paprika, and salt to taste, stirring constantly.

3. Add the cheese, a handful at a time, stirring constantly, until melted.

4. Serve piping hot and topped as desired.

Over the Fire

12" with lid

Use a camp-style Dutch oven on a rack instead.
Partially covering the pasta while it cooks, follow all steps above.

Spicy Chili Mac

Ingredients

- **1 pound ground beef**
- **1 onion, chopped**
- **2 (10 ounce) cans mild diced tomatoes with green chiles**
- **1 cup water**
- **1½ cup uncooked rotini pasta or elbow macaroni**
- **Seasoned salt and black pepper, to taste**
- **½ cup shredded cheddar cheese**

On the Stove

1. Place Dutch oven on stovetop over medium heat.
2. Cook the beef and onion until meat is brown and crumbly and onion is tender.
3. Stir in tomatoes with chiles, water, and pasta; sprinkle with seasoned salt and pepper as desired.
4. Bring mixture to a boil and cover pot with lid. Let simmer about 20 minutes or until pasta is tender. Stir after 15 minutes. Dish it up hot and sprinkle with cheese.

Over the Fire (20 hot coals)

1. Spread about 20 hot coals in a flat layer under the camp-style Dutch oven.
2. Cook the beef and onion until meat is brown and crumbly and onion is tender.
3. Stir in tomatoes with chiles, water, and pasta; sprinkle with seasoned salt and pepper as desired. Bring mixture to a boil and cover pot with lid.
4. Rearrange 7 of the hot coals in a ring under the Dutch oven and move remaining coals to the lid. Let simmer about 20 minutes or until pasta is tender.
5. Stir after 15 minutes and then rotate pot and lid to finish cooking. Dish it up hot and sprinkle with cheese.

TIP
When you begin to smell the food inside your Dutch oven, it's a sign the dish is almost ready to eat!

These tuna patties are packed with tons of flavor, and the sauce complements them perfectly! (Psst...Dip the sweet potato fries into the sauce, too. Yum!)

Tuna Patties with Dill Sauce

SERVES 2

Ingredients

- ¼ cup sour cream
- ¼ cup mayo
- 1 teaspoon dill weed
- 2 (6.4 ounce) pouches tuna
- ½ cup torn white bread
- 2 teaspoons Dijon mustard
- 1 teaspoon lemon zest
- 1 teaspoon lemon juice
- 2 tablespoons each chopped fresh parsley and chives

- Hot sauce, to taste
- Sea salt and black pepper, to taste
- 1 egg, beaten
- 1 teaspoon butter
- 1 tablespoon olive oil
- Sweet Potato Fries (see recipe on page 47), for serving

On the Stove

1. For the sauce, stir together the sour cream, mayo, and dill weed. Chill until serving.

2. Toss the tuna into a bowl and flake; add the bread. Stir in the mustard, lemon zest and juice, parsley, chives, and hot sauce. Season with salt and black pepper, then stir in the egg.

3. Divide the mixture into four even patties, place on a wax-paper-lined tray, and pat with paper towels to absorb excess liquid. Chill for an hour.

4. Melt the butter and oil together in a skillet over medium heat. Arrange the chilled patties in the hot oil and fry 6 to 7 minutes, until nicely browned and beginning to hold together; flip and fry until brown on the other side.

5. Drain on paper towels. Serve with the chilled sauce and Sweet Potato Fries.

Sweet Potato Fries

Ingredients

- ½ teaspoon steak seasoning
- ¼ teaspoon black pepper
- ¼ teaspoon garlic powder
- ⅛ teaspoon salt
- ⅛ teaspoon paprika
- 3 tablespoons olive oil, divided
- 2 sweet potatoes

On the Stove

1. Mix steak seasoning, pepper, garlic powder, salt, paprika, and 2 tablespoons olive oil. Peel sweet potatoes and cut into French fry shapes; drizzle with the seasoned oil and toss to coat.

2. Heat the remaining olive oil in a skillet over medium heat and add the fries in a single layer; cover and cook for 5 minutes.

3. Flip the fries, cover, and cook 5 minutes longer, until tender.

Tuna Noodle Casserole

Ingredients

- **1 cup uncooked egg noodles (I used kluski noodles)**
- **2 tablespoons butter, divided**
- **1 shallot, finely chopped**
- **Salt and black pepper, to taste**
- **1½ tablespoons flour**
- **¾ cup, plus 2 tablespoons chicken broth**
- **½ cup milk**
- **½ cup frozen peas**
- **¼ cup roasted red peppers, drained and chopped**
- **1 (5 ounce) can tuna packed in water, drained**
- **½ cup shredded sharp cheddar cheese**
- **2 tablespoons breadcrumbs**
- **¼ teaspoon dried dill weed**
- **2 tablespoons Parmesan cheese**

On the Stove and in the Oven

1. Preheat oven to 375°F. In a 10-inch oven-safe skillet, cook noodles to al dente according to package directions. Drain the noodles and dump into a bowl; toss with 1 tablespoon of the butter and set aside.

2. Melt the remaining 1 tablespoon butter in the same skillet over medium heat. Add the shallot and season with salt and black pepper; sauté 3 to 4 minutes, until softened, stirring occasionally.

3. Stir in the flour and heat 30 seconds or so. Slowly whisk in the broth, breaking up any lumps. Add the milk and bring the mixture to a boil over medium-high heat.

4. Stir in the peas, reduce heat to medium, and cook 5 minutes or until thickened, whisking often.

5. Stir in the roasted peppers and tuna and season again with salt and pepper. Remove the skillet from the heat and stir in the cheddar until melted, then stir in the set-aside noodles.

6. Combine the breadcrumbs, dill weed, and Parmesan and sprinkle evenly over the top of the tuna mixture.

7. Spritz the top with a hefty dose of cooking spray and bake uncovered 20 to 25 minutes or until bubbly and golden brown.

This tuna noodle casserole is w-a-y better than Mom used to make (sorry Mom). Roasted red peppers give it little kick, Parmesan adds a nutty flavor, and a handful of cheddar and a bit of dill weed just make everything better.

Veggie Bake

Ingredients

- **Water**
- **8 cups fresh vegetables, any combination (I used cauliflower, broccoli, carrots, mushrooms, onions, and butternut squash), chopped**
- **Garlic powder, salt, and black pepper, to taste**
- **¼ cup butter, sliced**
- **Grated Parmesan cheese, as needed**

On the Stove and in the Oven

1. Pour enough water into the pot of a 10-inch, kitchen-style Dutch oven to cover the bottom.
2. Add the vegetables, season generously with garlic powder, salt, and pepper, and set the pot over medium-high heat; bring to a boil.
3. Distribute the butter slices evenly over the top, cover the pot with the lid, and bake in a 350°F oven for 25 minutes or until vegetables are fork-tender.
4. Sprinkle with cheese and serve.

Over the Fire (24 hot coals)

1. Spread 24 hot coals in a flat layer. Pour enough water into the pot of a 10-inch camp-style Dutch oven to cover the bottom and set the pot on the hot coals.
2. Add the vegetables and season generously with garlic powder, salt, and pepper. Distribute the butter slices evenly over the top and cover the pot with the lid.
3. Cook for 10 to 15 minutes, until steam escapes from the lid. Remove about half the coals, and continue to cook until the vegetables are fork-tender.
4. Remove the lid and let the heat from under the pot help evaporate most of the remaining water.
5. Sprinkle with cheese and serve.

Apple-Cinnamon Grilled Cheese

SERVES 1

Ingredients

- **⅓ cup walnuts, chopped**
- **1 tablespoon honey**
- **2 ounces cream cheese, softened**
- **¼ teaspoon cinnamon**

- **2 slices cinnamon raisin bread**
- **Granny Smith or Golden Delicious apple, sliced**
- **1 slice cheddar cheese**
- **Butter, as needed**

On the Stove

12"

1. In a big skillet, cook and stir walnuts and honey over medium heat for several minutes, until hot and lightly toasted (watch closely so they don't burn).

2. In a small bowl, mix cream cheese with cinnamon; stir in the toasted walnuts and spread evenly over cinnamon raisin bread.

3. Top with several thin slices of apple, cheddar cheese, and another bread slice. Press gently.

4. Wipe out the skillet and heat over medium-low heat. Butter the outside of each sandwich and toast in the hot skillet a couple of minutes on each side, until golden brown and the cheese is melted. Serve alongside Pecan-Cranberry Brie (see recipe on page 53).

Pecan-Cranberry Brie

SERVES 8

Ingredients

- 1 (8 ounce) wheel Brie cheese, rind trimmed
- 2 tablespoons plus ¼ cup brown sugar
- 2 tablespoons honey
- 2 tablespoons maple syrup
- 1 tablespoon unsalted butter
- ¼ teaspoon ground cinnamon
- Pinch of ground nutmeg
- Zest of 1 orange
- ½ cup chopped pecans
- ¼ cup dried cranberries
- Your favorite crackers, for serving

On the Stove

9"

1. Place Brie in a small skillet and sprinkle with 2 tablespoons of the brown sugar. Bake in a 350°F oven for 12 to 15 minutes, until softened; let cool 5 minutes.

2. Meanwhile, in a separate skillet or small saucepan, combine the honey, syrup, butter, cinnamon, nutmeg, orange zest, and the remaining ¼ cup brown sugar.

3. Bring to a boil, reduce heat, and simmer a couple of minutes until foamy, stirring occasionally. Stir in pecans and dried cranberries; keep warm.

4. Serve warm Brie topped with the pecan mixture. Serve with crackers.

Over the Fire

9"

1. Place Brie in a small skillet and sprinkle with 2 tablespoons of the brown sugar. Set the skillet on a grate over hot coals, tent loosely with foil, and heat until softened; let cool 5 minutes.

2. Follow steps 2–4 above.

Italian Beef Stew

Ingredients

- ¾ pound beef stew meat, cut into bite-size pieces
- 1 cup water
- 1 (8 ounce) can tomato sauce
- 2 small red potatoes, cubed
- ½ cup sliced carrot
- ½ cup chopped onion
- ½ small red bell pepper, chopped
- ¼ cup celery, sliced
- 1 tablespoon dry beefy onion soup mix
- ½ teaspoon Italian seasoning
- ¼ teaspoon garlic powder
- Salt and black pepper, to taste
- ½ cup frozen peas

On the Stove

1. Coat a big skillet with cooking spray and heat over medium heat.

2. Add stew meat, cooking and stirring until brown.

3. Stir in water, tomato sauce, potatoes, carrot, onion, red bell pepper, celery, soup mix, Italian seasoning, garlic powder, and salt and black pepper.

4. Bring to a boil, then reduce heat and simmer uncovered 30 to 45 minutes, until thickened and the veggies are tender, stirring occasionally.

5. Stir in frozen peas and simmer until heated through. Serve and enjoy.

Thick & Hearty Beef Stew

SERVES 8

Ingredients

- 2 pounds cubed beef stew meat
- ¼ cup flour
- ½ teaspoon salt
- ½ teaspoon black pepper
- 1 tablespoon tomato paste
- 2½ cups beef stock
- 1 onion, chopped
- 3 potatoes, diced
- 4 carrots, sliced
- 1 celery rib, chopped
- 2 bay leaves, optional
- 1 teaspoon minced garlic
- 1 teaspoon paprika
- 1 teaspoon Worcestershire sauce
- Bread, for serving

On the Stove and in the Oven

10" with lid

1. Place the meat in the pot of a 10-inch kitchen-style Dutch oven.

2. Mix a generous ¼ cup flour with the salt and pepper and sprinkle over the meat; toss to coat.

3. Stir in the tomato paste, stock, onion, celery, bay leaves if using, garlic, paprika, and Worcestershire sauce.

4. Cover the pot and bake in a 350°F oven for 2¼ hours.

5. Add the potatoes and carrots. Cover and bake 1 hour longer or until meat and vegetables are tender.

6. To thicken the stew, simmer uncovered for 10 minutes to allow some of the liquid to cook off. Serve with bread and enjoy.

Over the Fire

10" with lid

1. Using a camp-style Dutch oven instead, follow steps 1–3 above.

2. Cover the pot and set on a grate over the fire or hang it on a tripod about 18 inches above hot coals.

3. Simmer about 4 hours, until meat and vegetables are tender, stirring occasionally, adjusting the heat or the distance from the coals as needed for slow, even cooking.

4. To thicken the stew, simmer uncovered for 10 minutes to allow some of the liquid to cook off. Serve with bread and enjoy.

Kielbasa Potato Chowder

Ingredients

- ½ pound kielbasa, cut into ½-inch chunks
- 4 bacon strips, diced
- 1 small onion, finely chopped
- ½ teaspoon minced garlic
- 1½ cups chicken broth
- 2 medium potatoes, cut into ½-inch chunks
- ½ teaspoon chicken bouillon granules or powder
- ¼ teaspoon black pepper
- 1 handful of torn kale leaves
- ½ cup heavy cream
- Sour cream and green onion, for serving (optional)

On the Stove

1. In a big skillet, brown the kielbasa and bacon; drain all but 1 teaspoon of the grease and set aside a little of the bacon for serving.

2. Add the onion to the skillet and sauté over medium heat for 3 minutes, until tender, stirring often. Add the garlic and cook for 30 seconds. Transfer the mixture to paper towels to drain.

3. Pour the broth into the same skillet, add 1½ cups water, and bring to a boil.

4. Add the potatoes, bouillon granules, and black pepper. Cook for 10 minutes or until tender.

5. Add the drained meat mixture and the kale to the skillet and heat over medium heat about 2 minutes, until the kale is wilted. Reduce the heat to low, add the cream, and stir a minute or two, until heated through.

6. For extra decadence, add a dollop of sour cream to each bowl of soup and sprinkle with some green onion and the set-aside bacon.

Ingredients

- ⅓ cup vegetable oil
- 8 corn tortillas, chopped
- 1 tablespoon minced garlic
- ½ cup chopped cilantro
- 1 onion, chopped
- 1 (28 ounce) can diced tomatoes, with liquid
- 1 (8.5 ounce) can whole kernel corn, with liquid
- 1 teaspoon onion salt
- 2 tablespoons ground cumin
- 1 tablespoon chili powder
- 6 cups chicken stock
- 4 cooked chicken breast halves, shredded
- 1 teaspoon salt
- ½ teaspoon cayenne pepper
- Monterey Jack cheese, avocado, and/or tortilla strips, for topping

Chicken Tortilla Soup

SERVES 6

On the Oven

1. In the pot of a 12-inch, kitchen-style Dutch oven, heat the oil over medium heat.
2. Add the tortilla pieces, garlic, cilantro, and onion and cook for a few minutes. Add the tomatoes and corn and bring to a boil.
3. Stir in the onion salt, cumin, and chili powder. Add the stock and return to a boil.
4. Reduce the heat and simmer for 30 minutes. Stir in the chicken, salt, and cayenne pepper.
5. Add toppings as desired.

Sweet Potato Black Bean Chili

SERVES 2

Ingredients

- 2 teaspoons olive oil
- 1 onion, diced
- 1 sweet potato, peeled and diced
- 1 teaspoon minced garlic
- 1 tablespoon chili powder
- 1½ teaspoons ground cumin
- ¼ teaspoon ground chipotle powder

- 1 teaspoon salt
- 1⅓ cups water
- 1 cup cooked (or canned) black beans, drained and rinsed
- 1 cup crushed tomatoes
- 2 teaspoons lime juice
- Sour cream, avocado, Manchego cheese, and cilantro, for topping

On the Stove

10"

1. Heat olive oil in a medium skillet over medium-high heat.

2. Add onion and sweet potato; sauté until the onion is slightly softened, stirring often. Add garlic, chili powder, cumin, chipotle powder, and salt; heat for 30 seconds, stirring constantly.

3. Add water and bring to a simmer; cover, reduce heat to maintain a gentle simmer, and cook for 10 minutes, until tender.

4. Stir in black beans, tomatoes, and lime juice; heat to simmering, stirring often. Cook until liquid is slightly reduced.

5. Top with sour cream, avocado, Manchego cheese, and cilantro.

Double Dutch Chili & Biscuits

Ingredients

- 1½ pounds lean ground beef
- 1½ pounds ground pork
- 1 onion, diced
- 8 cloves garlic, minced
- 1 green bell pepper, diced
- 1 (28 ounce) can diced tomatoes, with liquid
- 1 (15 ounce) can tomato sauce, with liquid
- 1 (16 ounce) can kidney beans, with liquid

- ½ teaspoon dried marjoram
- 2 to 3 tablespoons Mexican chili powder
- 1½ tablespoons Southwest chipotle seasoning
- 1 tablespoon ground cumin
- Salt and black pepper, to taste
- 1 (16.3 ounce) tube large, refrigerated buttermilk biscuits
- 3 tablespoons melted butter, divided

On the Stove and in the Oven

1. Cook the ground beef and pork in the pot of a 12-inch kitchen-style Dutch oven for 5 to 10 minutes.

2. Add onion, garlic, and bell pepper; cook until vegetables are softened and meat is cooked, crumbling it while it cooks. Stir in the tomatoes, tomato sauce, beans, and all the seasonings.

3. Cover the pot and bake in a 350°F oven for 45 minutes.

4. Arrange the biscuits in a greased 10-inch kitchen-style Dutch oven and brush with half the melted butter. Add the biscuits to the oven, remove the lid from the chili, and bake both for 15 to 20 minutes, until the biscuits are done, and the chili is thick.

5. Brush baked biscuits with the remaining melted butter and serve.

Over the Fire (20 hot coals)

1. Using a camp-style Dutch oven instead, follow steps 1–2 above.

2. Cover the pot and set on a ring of 12 hot coals with 8 hot coals on the lid. Simmer the chili about 40 minutes, rotating the pot and lid several times and adjusting coals to maintain a simmer.

3. Meanwhile, arrange the biscuits in a well-oiled 10-inch Dutch oven and brush with half the melted butter; set aside.

4. Move fresh coals to the lid of the 12-inch oven and stack the 10-inch oven on top with 8 to 10 coals on the lid.

5. Bake for 20 to 30 minutes, until biscuits are golden. Rotate the top pot and lid and replenish coals as needed, placing a few hot ones near the handle.

6. Brush baked biscuits with the remaining melted butter and serve.

SERVES
8

Calico Chili

Ingredients

- 1 pound lean ground beef
- ¾ cup chopped onion
- 1¾ cups bell peppers, cored, seeded, and chopped
- 1 teaspoon minced garlic
- 1 (16 ounce) can chili beans, with liquid
- 1 (16 ounce) can Northern beans, drained, rinsed
- 1 (14.5 ounce) can diced tomatoes, with liquid
- 1¼ cups tomato juice or V-8
- 1 ⅓ cups frozen or canned whole kernel corn, drained
- 1 (1 ounce) envelope ranch salad dressing mix
- Corn chips, for garnish (optional)
- Shredded cheddar cheese, for garnish (optional)
- Cornbread, biscuits, or sourdough bread, for serving

On the Stove

1. Place Dutch oven on stovetop over medium-high heat and add ground beef and onion. Cook and stir until meat is crumbly and lightly browned and onion is tender; drain.

2. Add garlic and bell peppers; cook for 3 minutes to soften.

3. Stir in 1 cup water, chili beans, Northern beans, tomatoes, tomato juice, corn, and dressing mix until well combined.

4. Bring to a simmer, stirring frequently. Reduce heat to low, cover and simmer slowly for 20 to 30 minutes, stirring occasionally, until flavors are blended.

5. Serve in bowls garnished with a few corn chips and cheese, if desired. Bake cornbread, biscuits, or sourdough bread to serve with chili.

Over the Fire or on the Grill (24 hot coals)

1. Spread hot coals in flat layer underneath camp-style Dutch oven.

2. Add ground beef and onion to pot. Cook and stir until meat is crumbly and lightly browned and onion is tender; drain.

3. Add garlic and bell peppers; cook for 3 minutes to soften. Stir in 1 cup water, chili beans, Northern beans, tomatoes, tomato juice, corn, and dressing mix until well combined. Bring to a simmer, stirring frequently. Cover pot with lid.

4. Rearrange about half of the hot coals to make cooking ring underneath Dutch oven; place remaining hot coals on lid. Simmer slowly for 20 to 30 minutes, stirring occasionally, until flavors are blended.

5. Rotate pot and lid once during cooking time and adjust the number of coals on top and bottom as needed for even cooking.

6. Serve in bowls garnished with a few corn chips and cheese, if desired. Bake cornbread, biscuits, or sourdough bread to serve with chili.

One-Pot Shells & Meatballs

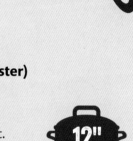

Ingredients

- 2 tablespoons vegetable oil
- 1 onion, chopped
- 2 celery ribs, thinly sliced
- 2 carrots, thinly sliced
- 1 teaspoon salt
- 1 teaspoon minced garlic
- 2 chicken bouillon cubes
- 3 cups chicken stock, divided
- 3 cups coarsely chopped fresh spinach
- 8 ounces uncooked large pasta shells
- 20 to 25 fully cooked frozen homestyle meatballs, thawed
- Shredded cheese of your choice (try Havarti, Romano, or Muenster)

On the Stove

1. Heat the oil in the pot of a kitchen-style Dutch oven over medium heat.

2. Add the onion, celery, and carrots and cook for 5 to 10 minutes or until softened, stirring occasionally.

3. Add the salt, garlic, bouillon cubes, and 1 cup of the stock; bring to a boil. Stir in the spinach, uncooked pasta, and the remaining 2 cups stock.

4. Return to a boil, cover, and simmer for 15 minutes, until the pasta is al dente; add the meatballs during the last 5 minutes of cooking time.

5. Remove the pot from the heat and sprinkle with cheese. Serve and enjoy.

Over the Fire

Using a camp-style Dutch oven instead, follow all steps above.

Ingredients

- **2 cups chopped grilled chicken**
- **¼ cup shredded Pepper Jack cheese**
- **1 cup shredded cheddar cheese**
- **1 (10.75 ounce) can cream of mushroom soup**
- **1 (10.75 ounce) can cream of celery soup**
- **1 (10 ounce) can diced tomatoes with green chiles**
- **¾ cup sliced green onions**
- **8 flour tortillas, cut into bite-size pieces**
- **½ cup shredded Colby Jack cheese**

Mexicali Pollo Bake

On the Stove and in the Oven

1. In the pot of a greased, 10-inch kitchen-style Dutch oven, mix the chicken, Pepper Jack and cheddar cheeses, both cans of soup, tomatoes with green chiles, green onions, and tortilla pieces.

2. Bake in a 350°F oven for 20 to 30 minutes, until hot and bubbly.

3. Sprinkle with the Colby Jack cheese; let set until melted.

Over the Fire or on the Grill (22 hot coals)

1. Using a camp-style Dutch oven instead, follow step 1 above.

2. Cover the pot and set on a ring of 11 hot coals with 11 more hot coals on the lid.

3. Cook 20 to 30 minutes or until hot and bubbly, rotating the pot and lid several times.

4. Sprinkle with the Colby Jack cheese; let set until melted.

Bacon & Beef Nachos

SERVES 6

Ingredients

- ½ pound bacon
- 1½ cups diced cooked roast beef
- 1 (15 ounce) can chili beans, partially drained
- ½ teaspoon salt
- ½ teaspoon black pepper
- 1 teaspoon chili powder
- 1 teaspoon onion powder
- Tortilla chips, as needed
- 2 cups shredded Mexican cheese blend
- Guacamole, jalapeños, sour cream, tomatoes, bell pepper, and/or salsa, for topping

On the Stove and in the Oven

10"

1. Cook the bacon in a medium skillet over medium-high heat; drain on paper towels and discard drippings from the skillet.
2. Meanwhile, heat the roast beef and chili beans until warm; stir in the salt, black pepper, chili powder, and onion powder.
3. Arrange a couple of handfuls of tortilla chips in the empty skillet; top with half the cheese, half the beef and bean mixture, and half the bacon; repeat layers.
4. Bake in a 400°F oven until the cheese melts and everything is hot.
5. Add your favorite toppings and enjoy.

Over the Fire

10"

1. Using a grate over a campfire instead, follow steps 1–3 above.
2. Cover the skillet and heat until the cheese melts and everything is hot.
3. Add your favorite toppings and enjoy.

Ingredients

- **2 pounds lean ground beef**
- **¾ cup coarsely chopped celery**
- **¾ cup coarsely chopped onion**
- **2 or 3 tomatoes, diced**
- **1½ cups ketchup**
- **¾ cup BBQ sauce**
- **1 (6 ounce) can tomato paste**
- **2 tablespoons apple cider vinegar**
- **Salt, black pepper, and garlic powder, to taste**
- **Slider buns and desired toppings, for serving**

SERVES 8

BBQ Sloppy Joe Sliders

On the Stove

1. Cook the ground beef in a big skillet over medium heat until browned, breaking it apart as it cooks.

2. Add the celery and onion and cook until tender; drain the grease from the skillet.

3. Stir in tomatoes, ketchup, BBQ sauce, tomato paste, and vinegar; season with salt, black pepper, and garlic powder. Let simmer until heated through, stirring often.

4. Spoon mixture onto buns and top as desired.

Over the Fire

Using a grate over a campfire instead, follow all steps above.

Cowboy Beans

Ingredients

- **8 ounces smoked sausage links**
- **2 tablespoons butter**
- **1½ cups chopped onion**
- **¾ cup BBQ sauce**
- **2 tablespoons maple syrup**
- **2 tablespoons apple cider vinegar**
- **¼ cup water**
- **1 (16 ounce) can each red kidney beans, black beans, and pinto beans**
- **Green onions, chopped, for garnish (optional)**

On the Stove

1. Slice smoked sausage links into ½-inch chunks and dump into a 10-inch or bigger skillet set over medium heat until evenly browned; remove sausages from the skillet.

2. Melt butter in the skillet and add chopped onion, cooking until softened.

3. Stir in BBQ sauce, maple syrup, apple cider vinegar, and water and bring to a boil.

4. Drain and rinse beans and add to the skillet along with the browned sausages; stir, cover the skillet, and simmer at least 15 minutes, stirring occasionally. Season with salt to taste.

5. Top with chopped green onions if you'd like. Serve with BBQ Slopy Joe Sliders (see recipe on page 68).

Over the Fire

Using a grate over a campfire instead, follow all steps above.

Ingredients

- **6 medium potatoes**
- **1 cup diced ham**
- **⅓ cup chopped onion**
- **⅓ cup diced bell pepper (any color)**
- **1 to 2 (10.7 ounce) cans cream of mushroom soup**
- **Onion salt, garlic powder, and black pepper, to taste**
- **¼ cup grated Parmesan cheese**

Rustic Ham & Potatoes

SERVES 8

Preparation

Thinly slice the potatoes into a bowl; rinse and drain.

In the Oven

1. Stir in the ham, onion, bell pepper, soup, and seasonings, and transfer to the pot of a greased 10-inch kitchen-style Dutch oven; cover with the lid.

2. Bake in a 375°F oven for 45 minutes or until tender.

3. Sprinkle with the cheese and cover until melted.

Over the Fire (22 hot coals)

1. Using a camp-style Dutch oven instead, follow steps 1–2 above.

2. Set the Dutch oven on a ring of 9 hot coals with 13 hot coals on the lid. Cook 35 to 40 minutes or until tender, rotating the pot and lid several times and allowing the coals to burn down.

3. Sprinkle with the cheese and cover until melted.

DINNER

These main dishes are hearty, delicious, and infused with the flavor of cast-iron. With every bite, you'll taste the smoky comfort of classic dishes—and new twists that you might not expect. Next time you build a fire, or even if you prefer to stay inside, and cook something that your guests will remember, flip to one of these recipes, and enjoy.

Chicken Enchilada Skillet

SERVES 2

Ingredients

- 1 (10 ounce) can tomatoes with green chiles
- 1 cup enchilada sauce
- 1 cup black beans, drained and rinsed
- 2 boneless, skinless chicken breast halves
- Salt, to taste
- 4 corn tortillas
- ½ cup shredded Monterey Jack cheese
- Green onion, avocado, tomatoes, and sour cream, for topping

On the Stove

10"

1. In a medium oven-safe skillet over medium heat, combine tomatoes with green chiles, enchilada sauce, and black beans; bring to a simmer.

2. Season chicken breast halves with salt; add to the skillet and cook over low heat for 20 minutes or until done, turning once.

3. Preheat your broiler. Shred the chicken and stir in tortillas, cut into bite-size pieces. Cover and simmer for 5 minutes.

4. Uncover, sprinkle with cheese, and broil a minute or two until the cheese melts. Serve topped with green onion, avocado, tomatoes, and sour cream, and alongside Hot Pimento Cheese Dip (see recipe on page 73).

Hot Pimento Cheese Dip

SERVES
8

Ingredients

- ½ cup mayonnaise
- ½ cup softened cream cheese
- 8 ounces shredded sharp cheddar cheese
- 8 ounces shredded Monterey Jack cheese
- 4 ounces pimentos
- 1 jalapeño, diced
- ¼ cup diced green onion
- 1 teaspoon ground cumin
- Cilantro
- Fresh vegetables and toast, for serving

Preparation

Beat the mayo and cream cheese until smooth. Stir in the cheddar, Monterey Jack, pimentos, jalapeño, green onion, and cumin.

On the Stove

9"

Spread the mixture evenly into a small skillet. Bake in a 350°F oven for 20 minutes or until hot and bubbly. Serve warm with vegetables and toast, and alongside Chicken Enchilada Skillet (see recipe on page 72).

Over the Fire

9"

Cover the skillet and set on a rack over hot coals until hot and bubbly. Serve warm with vegetables and toast, and alongside Chicken Enchilada Skillet (see recipe on page 72).

Fajita Enchiladas

Ingredients

- 2 tablespoons vegetable oil
- 1 red bell pepper, cut into strips
- ½ red onion, thinly sliced
- 2 teaspoons minced garlic
- 1 tablespoon ground cumin
- 2 teaspoons salt
- 1 (14 ounce) can enchilada sauce
- 1 (15 ounce) can black beans, drained and rinsed
- 2 cups shredded cheddar cheese
- 8 flour tortillas
- Sour cream, guacamole, avocado, and/or tomatoes, and/or Cast-Iron Salsa (see recipe on page 75) for topping

On the Stove and in the Oven

1. Heat the oil in the pot of a kitchen-style Dutch oven. Add the bell pepper and onion and sauté until onion is soft and translucent.

2. Stir in the garlic, cumin, and salt and keep on the heat for 30 seconds. Remove from the heat and transfer the vegetables to a plate.

3. Coat the bottom of the pot with ½ cup enchilada sauce.

4. Divide the pepper mixture, black beans, and half the cheese among the tortillas; roll up and place in a single layer, seam side down, in the pot. Cover the enchiladas with the remaining sauce and cheese. Cover the pot.

5. Bake in a 350°F oven for 10 to 15 minutes, until the cheese melts.

6. Add toppings as desired.

Over The Fire (24 hot coals)

1. Using a camp-style Dutch oven instead, follow steps 1–4 above.

2. Set the Dutch oven on a ring of 9 hot coals with 15 hot coals on the lid. Cook for 10 minutes, until the cheese is melted.

3. Add toppings as desired.

CAST-IRON SALSA

- 3 plum tomatoes
- 1 jalapeño
- 1 white onion
- 3 garlic cloves, unpeeled
- 1½ tablespoons lime juice
- ¾ teaspoon salt
- ⅓ cup cilantro, chopped

1. Heat a 12-inch skillet over medium heat.
2. Cut tomatoes and jalapeño in half lengthwise. Cut onion into thin wedges.
3. In batches without crowding the pan, lay vegetables cut side down; add garlic cloves. Cook until lightly charred.
4. Peel garlic and transfer everything to a food processor or blender. Process to desired consistency.
5. Add lime juice and salt. Cool, then stir in cilantro. Makes 1½ cups.

12"

Fruited Balsamic Chicken

Ingredients

- **2 tablespoons olive oil**
- **2 (5- to 6-ounce) boneless, skinless chicken breast halves**
- **½ cup chopped onion**
- **Salt and black pepper, to taste**
- **½ teaspoon minced garlic**
- **2½ tablespoons balsamic vinegar**
- **1½ teaspoons honey**
- **1 medium peach (ripe but still firm), sliced**
- **1 cup pitted sweet cherries**
- **Sliced fresh basil, for topping**

On the Stove

1. Heat the oil in a medium skillet over medium heat. Add the chicken breasts and dump the onion around the outer edge of the skillet; season with salt and pepper.

2. Fry the chicken a few minutes on each side, until golden brown, stirring the onion often. Transfer the chicken to a plate.

3. Add the garlic to the skillet with the onion and heat for 30 seconds. Stir in the vinegar and cook for 2 minutes, until the liquid is reduced by about half.

4. Stir in the honey, then add the peaches and cherries, tossing to coat.

5. Return the chicken and any accumulated juices to the skillet, nestling the pieces among the fruit; season everything with a little more salt and pepper.

6. Cover the skillet, reduce the heat to medium-low, and simmer 7 or 8 minutes, until the internal temperature of the chicken reaches 165°F. Top with basil and serve.

TIP
If peaches and cherries are out of season, just grab frozen ones—they work just as well in a pinch.

Ingredients

- **1 cup chicken broth**
- **2 tablespoons lime juice**
- **1 tablespoon minced garlic**
- **⅛ teaspoon ground cumin**
- **½ teaspoon red pepper flakes**
- **2 boneless, skinless chicken breast halves**
- **Salt and black pepper, to taste**
- **1 tablespoon olive oil**
- **⅓ cup finely chopped yellow onion**
- **2 tablespoons finely chopped jalapeño**
- **3 tablespoons butter**
- **¼ cup heavy cream**
- **Fresh cilantro, for topping**
- **Chopped tomato, for topping**

SERVES 2

Chicken with Firecracker Cream

On the Stove and in the Oven

10"

1. Position an oven rack in the lower third of the oven and preheat your oven to 375°F.

2. For the cream sauce, stir together the broth, lime juice, garlic, cumin, and pepper flakes; set aside.

3. Using a mallet, pound the chicken to ½-inch thickness; season both sides with salt and black pepper.

4. Heat the oil in a medium oven-safe skillet over medium-high heat. Add the chicken and brown on both sides, turning once; transfer to a plate.

5. Reduce the heat to medium and add the onion and set-aside sauce to the skillet, scraping to loosen any browned bits. Toss in the jalapeño and cook 10 to 12 minutes or until most of the liquid has evaporated.

6. Remove the skillet from the heat, add the butter, and whisk until melted.

7. Whisk in the cream and return the skillet to the heat until warm (but don't let the sauce boil). Remove from the heat and add the chicken, spooning sauce over the top.

8. Bake uncovered until the internal temperature of the chicken reaches 165°F. Serve the chicken with the sauce and top with cilantro and tomato. Serve with Jalapeño Cornbread (see recipe on page 79).

Jalapeño Cornbread

Ingredients

- **Vegetable oil, as needed, plus 2 teaspoons**
- **½ cup flour**
- **½ cup yellow cornmeal**
- **2 tablespoons shredded Mexican cheese blend**
- **Chopped jalapeño, to taste**

In the Oven

1. Preheat your oven to 425°F.

2. Pour enough vegetable oil into an 8-inch, oven-safe skillet to just cover the bottom; set into the oven.

3. Sift together flour, cornmeal, baking powder, salt; stir in egg, milk, 2 teaspoons vegetable oil, Mexican cheese blend, and chopped jalapeño to taste.

4. Pour into the hot skillet and bake for 15 minutes or until done. Serve with Chicken with Firecracker Cream (see page 78 for recipe).

Campfire Cola Chicken

SERVES 6

Ingredients

- **6 boneless, skinless chicken breast halves**
- **½ large onion, sliced**
- **1 (12 ounce) can cola**
- **1 (6 ounce) can tomato paste**
- **1 (5.5 ounce) can vegetable juice**
- **¼ cup water**
- **1½ teaspoon minced garlic**
- **1 tablespoon chili powder**

On the Stove and in the Oven

12"

1. Arrange chicken breast halves in a 12-inch skillet and char lightly over medium heat.

2. Add sliced onion to the skillet. Combine cola, tomato paste, vegetable juice, water, garlic, and chili powder and pour it over the chicken and onions.

3. Cover the skillet and bake in a 350°F oven about an hour, until the chicken is done (165°F).

4. Serve and enjoy.

Over The Fire (24 hot coals)

12" with lid

1. Using a camp-style Dutch oven instead, follow steps 1–2 above.

2. Cover the pot and set on a ring of 9 hot coals with 15 hot coals on the lid. Bake for 60 to 75 minutes, until the chicken is cooked through (165°F), rotating the pot and lid occasionally and replenishing coals as needed.

3. Serve and enjoy.

Roasted Potato Lineup

SERVES 6

Ingredients

- **6 medium red potatoes**
- **6 garlic cloves, minced**
- **1 tablespoon vegetable oil**
- **1 teaspoon Italian seasoning**
- **Coarse sea salt and black pepper, to taste**
- **½ cup butter, cubed**
- **¼ cup shredded Parmesan cheese**
- **Parsley, for garnish (optional)**

In the Oven

10"

1. Grease the bottom and sides of a 10-inch skillet with olive oil. Cut potatoes crosswise into ¼-inch-thick slices and put the slices into a big bowl.

2. Add garlic, vegetable oil, Italian seasoning, and coarse sea salt and black pepper; toss to coat.

3. Set the potato slices upright around the edge of the skillet and then fill in the center. Scrape any remaining oil and seasonings out of the bowl and onto the potatoes. Lay the butter cubes over the top.

4. Cover the skillet and bake in a 375°F oven for an hour, until the potatoes are tender.

5. Uncover, sprinkle with Parmesan cheese, and bake for 20 to 30 minutes more to crisp slightly.

6. Toss on some parsley if you'd like, then dig in and enjoy!

Over the Fire

10"

1. Follow steps 1–3 for above.

2. Cover the skillet and set on a rack over hot embers until the potatoes are tender.

3. Uncover, sprinkle with Parmesan cheese, and heat until melted.

4. Toss on some parsley if you'd like, then dig in and enjoy!

Avocado Caprese Chicken

Ingredients

- ¼ teaspoon each garlic powder and onion powder
- ¼ teaspoon Italian seasoning
- ½ teaspoon salt, plus more to taste
- ¼ teaspoon black pepper, plus more to taste
- 2 (5 to 6 ounce) boneless, skinless chicken breast halves
- 2 tablespoons olive oil
- Fresh mozzarella slices, as needed
- Avocado slices, as needed
- Tomato slices, as needed
- Balsamic vinegar, as needed

On the Stove

1. Stir together the garlic powder, onion powder, Italian seasoning, salt, and black pepper and sprinkle the mixture evenly over both sides of the chicken.

2. Heat the oil in a skillet over medium heat. Add the chicken, cover, and fry about 5 minutes, until golden brown on the bottom. Flip and fry, covered, 4 to 5 minutes more, until nearly cooked through (internal temperature should be about 160°F).

3. Turn off the heat, place mozzarella over each chicken portion, followed by avocado and tomato slices. Cover until the chicken reaches 165°F and the cheese melts.

4. Sprinkle with a little more salt and pepper and drizzle with vinegar. Serve and enjoy.

Chicken Marsala

SERVES 4

Ingredients

- 4 skin-on, bone-in chicken thighs
- Olive oil, as needed
- 3 tablespoons butter, divided
- 2 shallots, finely chopped
- 8 ounces fresh mushrooms, sliced
- 2 cloves garlic, finely chopped
- ½ cup Marsala cooking wine
- ½ cup heavy cream
- 1 teaspoon dried thyme
- Salt and black pepper, to taste

On the Stove and in the Oven

12"

1. Preheat your oven to 375°F.

2. Heat a big oven-safe skillet over medium-high heat. Brush the skin side of the chicken thighs with a little oil and place in the hot skillet, skin side down. Cook for 5 minutes or until nice and brown on the bottom, then transfer to a plate.

3. Wipe out any burned bits from the pan and add 2 tablespoons of the butter; when it's melted and has browned slightly, reduce the heat to medium and sauté the shallots for 5 minutes, stirring often.

4. Add the mushrooms and sauté 5 minutes longer, until beginning to brown, stirring often.

5. Add the garlic and cooking wine and increase the heat to medium-high until the liquid reduces a bit. Stir in the cream and thyme and season with salt and black pepper. Add the remaining 1 tablespoon butter and let it melt.

6. Return the chicken to the skillet, skin side up, and spoon some of the sauce over the top. Bake uncovered for 30 minutes or until the internal temperature of the chicken reaches 165°F.

Cheesy Puffed Potatoes

SERVES 12

Ingredients

- **4 pounds russet potatoes, peeled and cubed**
- **2 cups shredded cheddar or Swiss cheese, divided**
- **1¼ cups milk**
- **5 tablespoons butter, softened**
- **1 teaspoon seasoned salt**
- **2 eggs, beaten**

On the Stove and in the Oven

12" with lid

1. Preheat oven to 350°F. Meanwhile, place potatoes in Dutch oven and cover with water. Set on stovetop over medium heat and bring to a boil; cook until tender, about 20 minutes. Drain water and mash potatoes.

2. Stir in 1¾ cups cheese, plus the milk, butter, and seasoned salt. Cook and stir over low heat until cheese and butter are melted. Fold in eggs.

3. Cover Dutch oven and transfer to center rack in oven; bake for 25 to 30 minutes. Remove lid and sprinkle with remaining ¼ cup cheese.

4. Bake uncovered until golden brown, 5 to 10 minutes, and serve.

Over the Fire

(24 hot coals)

12" with lid

1. Spread most of the hot coals in a flat layer underneath Dutch oven. Add potatoes and cover with water. Cover pot with lid and cook until tender, 20 to 30 minutes. Drain water and mash potatoes.

2. Follow step 2 above.

3. Rearrange about one-third of the hot coals to make cooking ring underneath Dutch oven. Place remaining hot coals on lid. Cook for 25 to 30 minutes. Rotate pot and lid twice during cooking. Toward end of cooking time, remove coals from lid to make second ring around outside of pot.

4. Remove lid and sprinkle remaining ¼ cup cheese over potatoes. Cook until melted, 5 to 10 minutes and serve.

Citrus Chicken & Sprouts

Ingredients

- 4 boneless, skinless chicken thighs
- 1 tablespoon chopped fresh parsley
- 1 teaspoon minced garlic
- 1½ teaspoons stone-ground Dijon mustard
- ¼ teaspoon onion powder
- 2 tablespoons olive oil
- ½ lemon, juiced, plus ½ lemon, sliced
- Salt and black pepper, to taste
- 2 to 3 cups halved Brussels sprouts (about ½ to ¾ pound)
- 6 bacon strips, cooked and crumbled, for topping

Preparation

Put the chicken in a big bowl and add the parsley, garlic, mustard, onion powder, oil, lemon juice, salt, and black pepper and stir to coat. Refrigerate for at least 30 minutes.

On the Stove and in the Oven

1. Arrange the chicken in a 12-inch skillet and arrange the Brussels sprouts around the chicken pieces. Lay the lemon slices over the food.

2. Bake uncovered in a preheated 400°F oven for 30 to 35 minutes, until the chicken is cooked through (165°F or no longer pink in the middle).

3. For additional browning, set the pan of food under the broiler for a few minutes.

4. Top with a big handful of chopped cooked bacon and serve.

Over the Fire (15 hot coals)

1. Using a 12-inch, camp-style Dutch oven, follow step 1 above.

2. Cover the pot and set 15 hot coals on the lid.

3. Bake for 35 to 40 minutes, until the chicken is cooked through (165°F or no longer pink in the middle), rotating the pot and lid occasionally and replenishing coals as needed.

4. Top with a big handful of chopped cooked bacon and serve.

Ingredients

- 2 (10- to 12-ounce) bone-in, skin-on chicken breasts
- Coarse salt, garlic pepper, and Montreal chicken seasoning, to taste
- 2 tablespoons olive oil
- 1 cup cherry tomatoes
- 4 cups frozen vegetables, thawed (I used broccoli, carrots, pearl onions, and lima beans)

All-in-One Chicken & Veggies

SERVES 2

12"

On the Stove

1. Preheat your oven to 375°F.

2. Lift the skin away from the chicken without removing it and sprinkle salt, garlic pepper, and chicken seasoning liberally between the skin and meat; smooth the skin back in place.

3. Preheat a big oven-safe skillet over medium-high heat; add the oil and heat until it just begins to smoke.

4. Carefully add the chicken breasts, skin side down, and sear for 3 minutes, until nicely browned and crispy.

5. Flip the breasts over and transfer the skillet to the oven. Bake uncovered for 30 minutes or until the internal temperature of the chicken reaches about 155°F.

6. Arrange the tomatoes and other vegetables around the chicken, sprinkle everything with salt and garlic pepper, and bake 10 to 15 minutes longer, until the internal temperature of the chicken reaches 165°F and the vegetables are crisp-tender.

Cheesy Baked Corn

SERVES
8

Ingredients

- 1 (15.2 ounce) can cream-style corn
- 1 (15.2 ounce) can whole kernel corn, drained
- ½ cup cornmeal
- 1 teaspoon garlic salt
- ½ cup grated Parmesan cheese
- 1½ cups cheddar cheese, shredded
- 1 teaspoon baking powder
- ¼ to ½ cup vegetable oil
- 2 eggs, lightly beaten
- ½ teaspoon onion powder, optional

Preparation

1. In a large bowl, combine cream-style corn, whole kernel corn, cornmeal, garlic salt, Parmesan cheese, cheddar cheese, baking powder, and oil; mix well.

2. Add eggs and stir to blend. Stir in onion powder, if desired.

In the Oven

12"

1. Preheat oven to 350°F. Grease bottom and sides of Dutch oven with nonstick cooking spray.

2. Pour prepared corn mixture into pot and place on center rack in oven. Bake uncovered for 40 to 45 minutes or until lightly browned and heated through.

Over the Fire

10"
with lid

1. Grease bottom and sides of Dutch oven with nonstick cooking spray. Pour prepared corn mixture into pot and cover with lid.

2. Arrange about one-third of the hot coals in cooking ring underneath Dutch oven. Place remaining hot coals on lid. Cook for 35 to 45 minutes, rotating pot and lid several times during cooking and replenishing coals on top and bottom as needed to maintain temperature.

TIP
Add one 4-ounce can chopped green chiles for a little kick.

Family-Style Chicken & Rice

Ingredients

- 1 (10.75 ounce) can cream of chicken soup
- 1 (10.75 ounce) can cream of mushroom soup
- 1 cup sour cream
- 2 cups uncooked white rice
- ¾ cup chopped onion
- 6 fresh mushrooms, sliced
- 2 large carrots, peeled and sliced
- 1 tablespoon Worcestershire sauce
- 1 to 2 teaspoons garlic powder
- ½ teaspoon salt
- ½ teaspoon white pepper
- 1 teaspoon paprika
- 5 or 6 bone-in chicken breasts
- Vegetable oil, as needed

Preparation

1. In a large bowl, combine both cans of soup, sour cream, and 2 cups water; whisk until well blended.

2. Stir in rice, onion, mushrooms, carrots, Worcestershire sauce, and garlic powder; set aside.

3. In a small bowl, mix salt, pepper, and paprika; sprinkle evenly over chicken pieces.

In the Oven

1. Preheat oven to 325°F. Lightly grease bottom of Dutch oven with vegetable oil.

2. Transfer prepared rice mixture into pot and spread evenly; arrange chicken on top of rice.

3. Cover Dutch oven and place on center rack in oven. Cook 1¼ to 1½ hours or until chicken is cooked through and rice and vegetables are tender.

4. Let stand several minutes before serving family style with a large spoon.

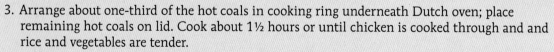

Over the Fire (28+ hot coals)

1. Lightly grease bottom of Dutch oven with vegetable oil.

2. Transfer prepared rice mixture into pot and spread evenly; arrange chicken on top of rice. Cover Dutch oven with lid.

3. Arrange about one-third of the hot coals in cooking ring underneath Dutch oven; place remaining hot coals on lid. Cook about 1½ hours or until chicken is cooked through and and rice and vegetables are tender.

4. Rotate pot and lid several times during cooking and replenish coals on top and bottom as needed to maintain cooking temperature.

5. Let stand several minutes before serving family style with a large spoon

Shepherd's Pie

Ingredients

- 3 medium white potatoes
- ¼ cup butter, softened
- ¼ cup milk
- ¾ cup shredded sharp cheddar cheese, divided
- 1½ teaspoon salt, divided
- 1 tablespoon vegetable oil
- ½ pound ground beef
- ½ cup chopped onion
- 1 teaspoon minced garlic
- ¾ cup tomato sauce
- 2 cups frozen peas and carrots combo
- ½ cup Guinness beer or water
- 1 tablespoon steak sauce
- 1 teaspoon dried thyme
- ½ cup beef broth

On the Stove and in the Oven

1. In a 9-inch oven-safe skillet, cook the potatoes in boiling water until tender but not mushy; drain well, transfer to a bowl, and mash.

2. Stir in the butter, milk, ½ cup cheddar, and 1 teaspoon salt; set aside and wipe out the skillet.

3. Heat the oil in the same skillet over medium heat; add the ground beef, onion, and garlic and cook until the meat is done, crumbling it while it cooks. Drain off the grease and return the meat to the skillet.

4. Add the tomato sauce and veggie combo and cook 4 to 5 minutes, stirring often. Pour in the beer and steak sauce; stir in the thyme and the remaining ½ teaspoon salt.

5. Bring to a boil, reduce heat, and simmer 10 minutes or until the liquid thickens and has reduced by about half. Add the broth and bring to a boil again; reduce the heat and simmer 20 to 25 minutes, until thick and glossy, stirring occasionally. Remove the skillet from the heat.

6. Preheat your oven to 350°F. Spread the set-aside mashed potato mixture evenly over the top of the food in the skillet and sprinkle with the remaining ¼ cup cheddar.

7. Bake 30 to 45 minutes, until everything is heated through, and the potatoes just start to brown.

8. Serve and enjoy!

Ingredients

- 1 (9 inch) refrigerated pie crust
- 1 cup sliced carrot coins
- ½ cup chopped onion
- 2 teaspoons minced garlic
- 1 (4 ounce) can sliced mushrooms, drained
- 1 cup frozen corn, partially thawed
- 1 cup frozen shredded hash browns, partially thawed
- ½ cup frozen peas, partially thawed
- 2 tablespoons olive oil
- Salt and pepper, to taste
- ½ teaspoon poultry seasoning, optional
- 3 cups chopped cooked chicken
- 1 (10.7 ounce) can cream of potato soup
- 1 (10.7 ounce) can cream of chicken soup
- ⅔ cup fat-free half and half

SERVES 8

Mama's Chicken Pot Pie

Preparation

1. Let pie crust stand at room temperature for 15 minutes (in wrapper).

2. In a medium bowl, combine carrots, onion, and garlic; in another bowl, combine mushrooms, corn, hash browns, and peas.

On the Stove and in the Oven

1. Preheat oven to 375°F. Meanwhile, place skillet on stovetop over medium heat and add oil.

2. When hot, add carrots and onion; sauté until crisp-tender. Stir in garlic and sauté briefly. Add mushrooms, corn, hash browns and peas, tossing to blend. Season with salt, pepper, and poultry seasoning as desired.

3. Cook about 2 minutes or until heated through, stirring frequently. Stir in chicken, both soups, and half and half; mix gently to blend. Cook until warmed.

4. Remove skillet from heat. Unroll crust and place over chicken filling to cover, crimping edges as needed. Cut several slits in crust to vent steam.

5. Place skillet on center rack in oven and bake for 40 to 45 minutes or until crust is golden brown and filling is bubbly. Let stand several minutes before serving in bowls, crust side up.

Cast-Iron Pizza with Sweet Potato Crust

SERVES 2

Ingredients

- 1 (8 to 10 ounce) sweet potato, peeled and cubed
- ⅔ cup old-fashioned oats
- 1 egg
- ¼ teaspoon onion powder
- ½ teaspoon salt
- Olive oil, as needed
- 1 cup shredded mozzarella cheese
- ⅓ cup pizza sauce
- Toppings of your choice (I used tomatoes, artichokes, mushrooms, black olives, red pepper flakes, and arugula)

Preparation

1. Preheat your oven to 400°F.
2. Toss the sweet potato and oats into a food processor and process until very finely chopped.
3. Add the egg, onion powder, and salt and process again until the mixture looks like thick batter.

In the Oven

10"

1. Transfer the batter to a 10-inch, parchment paper-lined cast-iron skillet and press flat with your hands until ½-inch thick.
2. Bake 25 to 30 minutes, until the top is dry to the touch. Brush around the edge of the crust with a little bit of oil and bake 5 to 10 minutes longer, until toasty brown.
3. Remove the skillet from the oven and scatter ¾ cup of the mozzarella over the crust; let stand until melted.
4. Add the sauce and any other toppings except arugula or other greens. Sprinkle the remaining ¼ cup cheese over the top.
5. Pop the skillet back into the oven and heat 5 to 10 minutes longer, until the cheese is melted, and the other toppings are warm.
6. You can slice the pizza right in the pan if you'd like, or, to make serving easier, lift it out using the ends of the paper, set on a cutting board, and then slice. Add the arugula just before serving.

Deep-Dish Pizza

Ingredients

- 18 frozen dinner rolls, thawed but still cold
- 1 (14 ounce) jar of your favorite pizza sauce, divided
- 1 teaspoon pizza seasoning
- ½ teaspoon Italian seasoning
- Pepperoni slices, as needed
- 1 onion, chopped
- 1 (2.25 ounce) can sliced black olives, drained
- Sliced mushrooms, as needed
- ½ yellow bell pepper, chopped
- ½ green bell pepper, chopped
- 1½ cups shredded provolone or mozzarella cheese

Preparation

1. Line a 12-inch kitchen-style Dutch oven with heavy-duty foil and coat the foil with cooking spray.

2. Cut each roll into 4 even pieces and toss them into the Dutch oven.

3. Stir in 1 cup of the pizza sauce and the seasonings, until rolls are coated; spread in a single layer. Drizzle with the remaining sauce and arrange the pepperoni over the top. Cover and let rise in a warm place for an hour.

In the Oven

1. Partially bake the pizza in a 450°F oven for 10 minutes. Add the onion, olives, mushrooms, and peppers.

2. Bake 12 to 15 minutes longer, until the crust is golden brown and no longer doughy.

3. Sprinkle pizza with cheese, cover, and let stand until cheese melts. Remove pizza from the pot by lifting the foil. Slice and serve.

Over the Fire (24 hot coals)

1. Set the camp-style Dutch oven on a ring of 10 to 12 hot coals with 12 hot coals on the lid. Cook 10 to 15 minutes.

2. Remove the lid and add onion, olives, mushrooms, and peppers. Cover and cook 20 to 30 minutes more or until crust is done, rotating the pot and lid several times and replenishing coals as needed.

3. Sprinkle pizza with cheese, cover, and let stand until cheese melts. Remove pizza from the pot by lifting the foil. Slice and serve.

Ingredients

- ¾ pound eggplant
- 1½ teaspoons coarse salt
- 1 egg
- 3 tablespoons milk
- ½ cup dry Italian breadcrumbs
- 1 tablespoon vegetable oil, plus more as needed
- About 1½ cups marinara sauce
- 2 cups shredded mozzarella cheese
- 1 cup shredded Parmesan cheese

SERVES 4

Eggplant Parmesan

In the Oven

10"

1. Cut the eggplant into ¼-inch-thick slices, sprinkle both sides with salt, and place into a large colander. Let drain 45 to 60 minutes, then brush off the excess salt.

2. In a shallow bowl, whisk together the egg and milk; dump the breadcrumbs into a separate bowl. Dip both sides of the eggplant slices into the egg mixture, then in the breadcrumbs, shaking off the excess. Set the slices on a tray.

3. Preheat your oven to 375°F. Heat 1 tablespoon oil in a 10-inch oven-safe skillet over medium heat.

4. Add eggplant slices to the hot oil a few at a time and fry until golden brown on both sides, turning once; transfer to paper towels. Repeat with the remaining eggplant slices, adding a little more oil to the skillet as needed. Remove the skillet from the heat and wipe it out after frying is complete.

5. Spread ½ cup marinara sauce in the skillet; add one-third of the breaded eggplant slices. Spread an additional ½ cup marinara sauce over the eggplant and sprinkle with ⅔ cup mozzarella and ⅓ cup Parmesan.

6. Repeat eggplant, sauce, and cheese layers two more times; press down lightly. Bake 20 to 25 minutes or until the cheese is bubbly. For extra browning, broil a minute or two at the end of baking.

Rustic Sage & Sausage Pasta

SERVES 4

Ingredients

- 1 tablespoon olive oil
- ½ pound sage-flavored sausage
- 1 red bell pepper, chopped
- 1 tomato, chopped
- 1 teaspoon chili powder
- ½ teaspoon minced garlic
- 2 tablespoons sundried tomato pesto
- 6 chopped fresh sage leaves (or 1 teaspoon dried sage)
- ¼ pound uncooked penne pasta
- 1 cup tomato sauce
- Shredded Manchego cheese, for topping

On the Stove

1. Heat olive oil in a 10-inch skillet over medium heat.
2. Add sausage and fry until done, crumbling it while it cooks. Add red bell pepper, tomato, chili powder, garlic, pesto, sage leaves, uncooked penne pasta, tomato sauce, and enough water to just cover everything.
3. Bring to a boil, then boil gently for 15 minutes, until the pasta is al dente, stirring occasionally.
4. Let stand 10 minutes, until most of the liquid is absorbed. Top with a handful of shredded Manchego cheese. Serve and enjoy.

SERVES 2

Ingredients

- ⅓ cup cottage cheese
- 1 egg yolk
- 1½ tablespoons heavy cream
- ⅛ teaspoon cornstarch
- ⅓ cup shredded Parmesan cheese, divided
- 3 ounces fresh mozzarella cheese, diced, divided
- ¼ pound uncooked spaghetti noodles, broken in half
- 1 (15 ounce) can pasta sauce (or Pasta Sauce for Two, see recipe on page 101)
- 4 rolls from a package of frozen garlic butter rolls
- 12 frozen meatballs, partially thawed

Garlic Rolls with Spaghetti & Meatballs

9"

On the Stove and in the Oven

1. Preheat your oven to 350°F.

2. In a bowl, stir together the cottage cheese, egg yolk, cream, cornstarch, 2 tablespoons Parmesan, and 2 ounces mozzarella.

3. Cook the noodles in a 9-inch oven-safe skillet until al dente, according to package directions; drain and dump them into the bowl with the cheese mixture.

4. Set aside 1 cup of the pasta sauce and stir the remainder into the noodle mixture.

5. Dry out the skillet and spritz with cooking spray; arrange the frozen rolls around the edge on one side, place the meatballs around the edge on the other side, and put the noodle mixture in the middle.

6. Drizzle the meatballs and noodles with set-aside sauce and toss the remaining 1 ounce mozzarella over the spaghetti.

7. Bake 20 to 25 minutes, until heated through. Sprinkle on the remaining Parmesan, cover with foil, and set aside 10 minutes to let the cheese melt.

Pasta Sauce for Two

Ingredients

- ½ chopped onion
- 2 tablespoons olive oil
- 1 teaspoon minced garlic
- 1 (15 ounce) can crushed tomatoes
- 2 tablespoons tomato paste

- ⅛ teaspoon dried oregano
- ⅛ teaspoon dried thyme
- ¾ teaspoon dried basil
- Salt and black pepper, to taste

On the Stove

1. Sauté chopped onion in hot olive oil in a small skillet over medium heat for 5 minutes, stirring often.

2. Add garlic and heat 1 minute longer. Stir in crushed tomatoes, tomato paste, dried oregano, dried thyme, dried basil, and salt and black pepper.

3. Bring to a boil, then reduce heat and simmer 10 minutes; longer for deeper flavor.

4. Serve with Garlic Rolls with Spaghetti & Meatballs (see page 100 for recipe).

Stovetop Skillet Lasagna

Ingredients

- ½ (12 ounce) package frozen veggie crumbles, partially thawed
- ½ sweet onion, diced
- 2 teaspoons minced garlic
- ½ (28 ounce) can crushed tomatoes
- 3 or 4 mushrooms, coarsely chopped
- 1¼ teaspoons salt
- ½ teaspoon black pepper
- ¼ cup ricotta cheese
- 1 egg, beaten
- 1½ tablespoons chopped fresh basil, plus more for garnish
- ½ (9 ounce) package oven-ready lasagna noodles, broken to fit
- 1¼ cups shredded provolone cheese
- Shredded Romano cheese, for topping

On the Stove

1. Mix the crumbles, onion, garlic, tomatoes, mushrooms, salt, and black pepper in a bowl. In a separate bowl, mix the ricotta, egg, and 1½ tablespoons basil.

2. Spread a little of the tomato mixture over the bottom of a 9-inch skillet; cover with half the ricotta mixture and half the noodles. Add the remaining ricotta, more of the tomato mixture, and the remaining noodles.

3. Cover with the remaining tomato mixture and drizzle with 2 tablespoons water; bring to a boil over medium-high heat.

4. Reduce heat to low, cover, and simmer 20 to 25 minutes or until noodles are tender.

5. Remove from the heat and top with provolone; cover and set aside until cheese melts. Top with Romano and sprinkle more basil over the lasagna before serving if you'd like.

6. Serve with Garlic Bread Bites (see recipe on page 104).

9"

SERVES
4

Garlic Bread Bites

SERVES 6

Ingredients

- **24 frozen rolls**
- **¾ cup butter**
- **1 tablespoon garlic salt**
- **1 tablespoon Italian seasoning, plus more as needed**
- **1 cup shredded Pepper Jack cheese, plus more as needed**
- **1 cup shaved Parmesan cheese, plus more as needed**

Preparation

1. Thaw rolls, but don't let them rise. In a 12-inch kitchen-style Dutch oven, melt butter; swirl it around to grease the sides.

2. Stir in garlic salt, Italian seasoning, and cheeses.

3. Cut each dough piece into fourths, add them to the pot, and toss to coat; arrange evenly.

In the Oven

1. Cover and bake in a 325°F oven for 35 minutes or until the edges are brown and dough is cooked through. Sprinkle on a little more cheese and Italian seasoning; cover until the cheese melts.

2. Serve hot, dipped in warm marinara sauce.

Over the Fire (40 hot coals)

1. Cover a camp-style Dutch oven and set on a ring of 17 hot coals with 23 hot coals on the lid.

2. After 30 minutes, rotate the pot and lid. Sprinkle on a little more cheese and Italian seasoning and bake 10 minutes more or until the edges are brown and dough is cooked through.

3. Serve hot, dipped in warm marinara sauce.

Pepperoni Mushroom Rigatoni

SERVES 4

Ingredients

- ½ pound Italian sausage
- 1½ cups spaghetti sauce
- 1 (4 ounce) can sliced mushrooms, drained
- 1 cup uncooked rigatoni pasta
- Water, as needed
- Pepperoni slices, as needed
- ¾ cup shredded Italian cheese blend

On the Stove and in the Oven

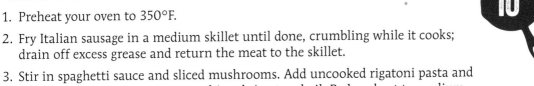

10"

1. Preheat your oven to 350°F.

2. Fry Italian sausage in a medium skillet until done, crumbling while it cooks; drain off excess grease and return the meat to the skillet.

3. Stir in spaghetti sauce and sliced mushrooms. Add uncooked rigatoni pasta and enough water to just cover everything; bring to a boil. Reduce heat to medium and cook for 15 minutes, until pasta is al dente.

4. Add a layer of pepperoni slices and cheese blend. Cover with greased foil and bake 25 to 30 minutes or until heated through.

5. Let stand 10 minutes before serving.

Wonton Lasagna

Ingredients

- ½ pound ground beef
- ½ pound Italian sausage
- 1 (4.25 ounce) can chopped black olives, optional
- 1 (12 ounce) tub cottage cheese
- ½ cup grated Romano cheese
- 1 egg
- 1 tablespoon dried parsley
- ½ teaspoon garlic powder
- 1 (24 ounce) jar marinara sauce
- 21 wonton wrappers
- 2 ¼ cups shredded mozzarella cheese

On the Stove and in the Oven

1. In the pot of a 10-inch kitchen-style Dutch oven, cook the ground beef and sausage over medium heat until browned, crumbling it while it cooks; drain.

2. Transfer the meat to a big bowl and cool slightly. Stir in black olives if using, cottage cheese, Romano cheese, egg, parsley, and garlic powder.

3. Spread about one-fourth of the marinara sauce over the bottom of the pot. Layer on 7 wonton wrappers, followed by half the meat mixture; top with about ½ cup sauce and ¾ cup mozzarella cheese. Repeat with another layer of wrappers, meat, sauce, and mozzarella. Top with 7 more wrappers and all the remaining sauce.

4. Cover the pot and bake in a 350°F oven for 20 to 30 minutes, until hot and bubbly; uncover, sprinkle the remaining ¾ cup mozzarella over the lasagna, and bake 10 minutes more to melt the cheese.

5. Let set for 15 minutes before serving.

Over the Fire (22 hot coals)

1. Using a camp-style Dutch oven instead, follow steps 1–3 above.

2. Cover the pot and set on a ring of 11 hot coals with 11 hot coals on the lid. Cook for 20 to 30 minutes, until hot and bubbly, rotating the pot and lid twice and replenishing the coals as needed.

3. Sprinkle the remaining ¾ cup mozzarella over the lasagna, cover, add some coals to the lid, and cook 10 minutes more to melt the cheese.

4. Let set for 15 minutes before serving.

ASIAN WONTON LASAGNA

Use these ingredients instead, following directions on page 106:

- 1 pound ground pork
- 2 green onions, thinly sliced
- 1 teaspoon minced garlic
- 1 tablespoon fresh gingerroot, finely chopped
- 1 (15 ounce) tub ricotta cheese
- 1½ cups shredded Parmesan cheese, divided
- 42 wonton wrappers
- 15 ounces tomato sauce
- 1 tablespoon fish sauce
- 1 tablespoon chili garlic sauce

Cook together pork, green onions, garlic, and fresh gingerroot; add ricotta cheese and 1 cup Parmesan cheese; double layers of wonton wrappers; tomato sauce with fish sauce and 1 tablespoon chili garlic sauce. Top with ½ cup shredded Parmesan. Serves 4.

Ingredients

- **4 strips bacon, chopped**
- **4 small zucchini, diced**
- **2 big handfuls cherry tomatoes, halved**
- **Salt and black pepper, to taste**
- **4 cups uncooked small shell pasta**
- **2 (14.5 ounce) cans vegetable broth**
- **½ cup purchased basil pesto**
- **½ cup grated Parmesan cheese, plus more for serving**
- **¼ cup pine nuts**

SERVES 4

Parmesan-Pesto Pasta

On the Stove

1. Place the bacon in the pot of a 10-inch kitchen-style Dutch oven over medium heat and cook until crispy; drain and set aside.

2. To the pot, add the zucchini, cherry tomatoes, and a big pinch of salt and sauté until the zucchini is tender and beginning to brown. Remove the vegetables to a bowl and set aside.

3. Dump the pasta into the empty pot and add the broth and 1 teaspoon salt; bring to a boil and cook until the pasta is tender and most of the liquid is absorbed, stirring often.

4. Remove the pot from the heat and stir in the pesto, Parmesan, nuts, and the set-aside bacon and vegetables. Season with salt and pepper.

5. Top with more Parmesan and serve with Italian Pesto Rolls (see recipe on page 110).

10"

Over the Fire

Using a camp-style Dutch oven instead, follow all steps above.

10" with lid

Fettuccine Primavera

SERVES 4

Ingredients

- ¼ pound fettuccine noodles
- 1 tablespoon butter
- 1½ cups thinly sliced fresh vegetables (I used red bell pepper, carrots, and zucchini)
- 1½ cups heavy cream
- ⅓ cup frozen peas, thawed
- Salt, black pepper, and cayenne pepper, to taste
- 1 cup shredded Italian cheese blend
- Fresh parsley and chives, for garnish
- Sunflower nuts, optional

On the Stove

12"

1. In a big skillet, cook fettuccine noodles according to package directions; drain, setting aside ½ cup of the cooking liquid.

2. In the same skillet over medium heat, melt butter.

3. Add the set-aside cooking liquid and fresh vegetables; cover and cook over medium-low heat for 3 minutes, until the vegetables are just tender.

4. Add heavy cream, peas, and salt, black pepper, and cayenne pepper; bring to a simmer.

5. Toss the set-aside noodles with the vegetables and add Italian cheese blend; simmer until the cheese melts and the sauce thickens.

6. Serve immediately sprinkled with fresh parsley and chives. Toss on some toasted sunflower nuts for added crunch if you'd like.

Italian Pesto Rolls

Ingredients

- 1 (16 ounce) package Pillsbury Hot Roll Mix
- 2 tablespoons, plus ¼ cup butter, softened and divided
- 1 egg
- Flour, for kneading
- ⅔ cup grated Parmesan cheese
- 1½ teaspoons garlic powder
- 2 teaspoons Italian seasoning
- ½ teaspoon dried oregano
- Sun-dried tomato pesto

Preparation

1. Following directions on roll mix package, mix contents of box and yeast in a large bowl. Stir in 1 cup hot water, 2 tablespoons butter, and egg until dough forms.

2. On floured surface, shape dough into a ball and knead until smooth, about 5 minutes.

3. Cover dough with large bowl and let rest 5 minutes. Meanwhile, in a small bowl, stir together Parmesan cheese, garlic powder, Italian seasoning, and oregano; set aside.

4. Roll dough into an 8 inch by 18 inch rectangle. Spread remaining ¼ cup butter and the pesto over dough. Sprinkle evenly with cheese mixture.

5. Starting at one long edge, roll up dough cinnamon-roll fashion and pinch long edge to seal. Cut into rolls about 1½" thick. Serve with Parmesan-Pesto Pasta (see recipe on page 109).

In the Oven

1. Grease bottom and lower sides of Dutch oven with nonstick cooking spray. Arrange rolls in a single layer in pot; cover with a cloth and let rise in a warm place until doubled in size, 30 to 40 minutes.

2. Preheat oven to 350°F. Remove cloth and bake uncovered for 25 to 30 minutes, or until lightly browned.

3. Allow rolls to cool in oven for several minutes before removing and serving.

Over the Fire (26 hot coals)

1. Arrange about one-third of the hot coals in cooking ring underneath a 12-inch camp-style Dutch oven and place remaining hot coals on lid.

2. Cook for 18 to 25 minutes or until lightly browned.

3. Rotate pot and lid twice during cooking and transfer most of the hot coals from bottom ring to lid toward end of cooking time to promote browning on top.

4. Allow rolls to cool in oven for several minutes before removing and serving.

TIP
Use thread or unflavored dental floss to slice rolls easily and maintain round shape.

Salisbury Steak

SERVES 2

Ingredients

- ½ pound lean ground beef
- 3 tablespoons dry breadcrumbs
- 2 teaspoons ketchup, divided
- 1 teaspoon Worcestershire sauce, divided
- ½ teaspoon yellow mustard
- ¼ teaspoon each garlic powder and onion powder
- 1 teaspoon vegetable oil
- 2 cups beef broth
- ¼ cup flour
- Salt and black pepper, to taste

On the Stove and in the Oven

10"

1. Mix the ground beef, breadcrumbs, 1 teaspoon ketchup, ½ teaspoon Worcestershire sauce, mustard, garlic powder, and onion powder; form two oval patties.

2. Heat the oil in a small skillet over medium heat and fry the patties until done to your liking, flipping to brown both sides. Transfer the patties to a plate and tent with foil.

3. Discard all but 3 tablespoons of the liquid from the skillet; add the broth to the skillet and bring to a light boil.

4. Transfer 1 cup of the liquid to a bowl and add the flour; whisk vigorously until smooth. Slowly whisk the flour mixture into the liquid in the skillet.

5. Add the remaining 1 teaspoon ketchup, ½ teaspoon Worcestershire sauce, and salt and black pepper. Whisk while simmering to form a thick gravy.

6. Return the patties to the skillet to reheat if desired, and serve the patties with the gravy. Serve with Garlic Mashed Potatoes (see recipe below).

Garlic Mashed Potatoes

Ingredients

- 4 cups water
- 2 large russet potatoes, peeled and sliced
- ½ teaspoon garlic powder
- ½ teaspoon salt
- ¼ teaspoon black pepper
- ¼ cup unsalted butter, softened
- ⅓ cup half and half

On the Stove

10"

1. In a deep skillet, boil water and add potatoes.

2. Cook for 10 minutes or until tender; drain and then mash.

3. Stir in garlic powder, salt, black pepper, and butter. A little at a time, stir in half and half, until desired consistency.

4. Serve with Salisbury Steak (see recipe above).

GARLIC MASHED POTATOES

Homestyle Pot Roast

SERVES 4

Ingredients

- 1 (4 to 5 pound) beef chuck roast
- Salt, black pepper, and garlic powder, to taste
- 2 to 3 tablespoons olive oil
- 2 (10.5 ounce) cans beef consommé
- 1 cup water
- 10 medium carrots, peeled, cut into 1-inch pieces
- 3 pounds medium golden potatoes, cut into 2-inch chunks
- 2 celery ribs, cut into 2-inch lengths
- 1 cup onion, chopped

Preparation

1. Season roast generously with salt, black pepper, and garlic powder.

2. Heat the oil in the pot of a deep 12-inch kitchen-style Dutch oven over medium-high heat.

3. Add the roast and brown on all sides; reduce heat to medium-low. Add the consommé and water.

On the Stove or in the Oven

1. Cover the pot and simmer slowly for 1½ to 2 hours or bake in a 350°F oven for 1½ to 2 hours.

2. Add the carrots, potatoes, celery, and onion to the pot. Cover and cook about 1 hour longer or until everything is tender.

3. Let meat stand a few minutes before slicing.

Over the Fire (About 20 hot coals)

1. Cover the camp-style Dutch oven and simmer slowly for 1½ to 2 hours, with a few hot coals on the bottom and a few more on the lid.

2. Add the carrots, potatoes, celery, and onion to the pot. Cover and set on a ring of 8 hot coals with 8 more on the lid.

3. Cook 1 hour longer or until everything is tender, replenishing coals as needed.

4. Let meat stand a few minutes before slicing.

Corned Beef & Cabbage

SERVES 6-8

Ingredients

- 1 pound bacon strips, chopped
- 1 small head green cabbage, cut into ½-inch-thick strips
- ⅓ cup water, plus more as needed
- 1 red onion, chopped
- 1 or 2 poblano peppers
- 1 green bell pepper, sliced
- 1 red bell pepper, sliced
- 1 (10.75 ounce) can cream of mushroom soup
- 1 teaspoon yellow mustard
- 12 ounces corned beef or pastrami, chopped
- 1 teaspoon garlic powder
- Salt and black pepper, to taste

On the Stove  12"

1. Fry the bacon in a 12-inch skillet until golden brown; do not drain.

2. Add some cabbage and ⅓ cup water; cover and cook a few minutes. Stir and add more cabbage as there is room, adding more water if the skillet becomes dry.

3. When the cabbage starts to wilt, stir in the onion, poblano peppers, bell peppers, soup, mustard, and corned beef; add a little water to thin the broth. Season with garlic powder, salt, and pepper.

4. Cover and cook about 15 minutes or until sauce is smooth and thick, stirring occasionally.

Over the Fire 12"

Using a grate over hot coals instead, follow all steps above.

Ingredients

- 1 (6 ounce) can pineapple juice
- 2 tablespoons chicken broth
- 1 tablespoon brown sugar
- 1 tablespoon soy sauce
- ⅛ teaspoon cayenne pepper
- ½ pound top sirloin steak, cut into thin bite-size strips
- 1 tablespoon cornstarch
- ¾ teaspoon olive oil, divided
- Salt, to taste
- 1 carrot, thinly sliced on the diagonal
- ½ small onion, chopped
- 1 small green bell pepper, thinly sliced
- ½ cup sugar snap peas
- ½ cup sliced fresh mushrooms
- ⅓ cup unsweetened pineapple chunks
- Sesame seeds, for garnish

SERVES 4

Pineapple Beef Stir Fry

12"

On the Stove

1. For the marinade, in a small bowl, whisk together the pineapple juice, broth, brown sugar, soy sauce, and cayenne pepper; transfer ⅓ cup to a big zippered plastic bag and chill the remainder. Add the steak to the bag, zip closed, and turn to coat; chill about an hour.

2. Drain and discard the marinade from the bag. In a small bowl, whisk together the cornstarch and reserved marinade until smooth; set aside.

3. In a big skillet, fry the steak in ½ teaspoon hot oil for several minutes, until no longer pink. Transfer steak to a plate, season with salt, and cover with foil.

4. Sauté the carrot and onion for 4 minutes. Add the remaining ¼ teaspoon oil, bell pepper, snap peas, and mushrooms and sauté 3 to 4 minutes more, until crisp-tender.

5. Whisk the cornstarch mixture again and add it to the skillet; bring to a boil, stirring constantly for 2 minutes or until thickened.

6. Stir in the pineapple and set-aside steak to heat through. Sprinkle with sesame seeds and serve.

Pan-Seared Steak

SERVES 4

Ingredients

- 2 tablespoons butter
- 2 tablespoons olive oil
- 4 sprigs fresh thyme
- 1 clove garlic, thinly sliced
- 4 (5 ounce) beef tenderloin steaks (about 1½-inch thick)
- Sea salt and black pepper, to taste
- ½ onion, cut into thin wedges
- 1 pound button mushrooms, quartered
- ½ cup dry red wine or unsweetened cranberry juice
- ½ cup beef broth
- ¼ cup whipping cream
- 2 teaspoons Dijon mustard

On the Stove and in the Oven

10"

1. Heat the butter, oil, thyme, and garlic in a big skillet over medium-high heat.
2. Season steaks with sea salt and pepper and add to the skillet; sear until browned on each side, turning once. Transfer steaks to a plate and set aside.
3. Add the onion to the skillet and cook until tender. Add the mushrooms and cook until softened, stirring often.
4. Pour in the wine and broth and simmer until the liquid is reduced by half. Stir in the whipping cream and mustard and return the steaks to the skillet.
5. Bake in a 400°F oven until steaks reach desired doneness (145°F for medium-rare). Serve steaks with the pan sauce.

Over the Fire

10"

1. Using a grate over a campfire instead, follow steps 1–4 above.
2. Cover the skillet and cook until steaks reach desired doneness (145°F for medium-rare). Serve steaks with the pan sauce.

Chops with Roasted Veggies

SERVES 2

Ingredients

- 1 yellow squash, cut into ½-inch slices
- 1 zucchini, cut into ½-inch slices
- 1 red bell pepper, cut into ½-inch slices
- ½ red onion, cut into ½-inch slices
- ¼ cup plus 2 tablespoons olive oil
- 2 tablespoons balsamic vinegar
- Salt and black pepper, to taste
- 2 (1-inch-thick) bone-in pork chops

On the Stove and in the Oven

12"

1. Preheat your oven to 425°F.

2. In a bowl, combine yellow squash, zucchini, red bell pepper, and red onion.

3. Add ¼ cup olive oil, balsamic vinegar, and salt and black pepper, stirring to coat; set aside.

4. Heat 2 tablespoons olive oil in a big oven-safe skillet over medium-high heat.

5. Add pork chops and sear 2 to 3 minutes or until nice and brown. Flip the chops over, season with salt and black pepper, and remove from the heat.

6. Arrange the veggies around the chops and bake uncovered 15 to 20 minutes, until the internal temperature of the chops reaches 145°F and veggies are beginning to brown around the edges. Let stand 3 minutes before serving.

Turkey Tenders Deluxe

SERVES 4

Ingredients

- ½ cup mayo
- ⅔ cup grated Parmesan cheese
- ½ teaspoon seasoned salt
- ¼ teaspoon black pepper
- ½ teaspoon garlic powder
- 2 (5 to 6 ounce) boneless turkey tenderloins
- Horseradish mayonnaise, for garnish (optional)

10"

In the Oven

1. Preheat your oven to 375°F.

2. In a bowl, mix mayo, Parmesan, salt, black pepper, and garlic powder and spread evenly over the top of the turkey tenderloins.

3. Set the tenderloins in a lightly greased oven-safe skillet and bake uncovered 35 to 45 minutes or until the internal temperature reaches 165°F.

4. Delicious on their own, but add a drizzle of horseradish mayo for a nice little added kick.

Turkey & Stuffing for Two

Ingredients

- **4 teaspoons olive oil, divided**
- **1 onion, chopped**
- **2 celery ribs, sliced**
- **Salt and black pepper, to taste**
- **4 corn muffins (homemade or purchased), crumbled**
- **2 tablespoons chopped fresh sage (or 2 teaspoons dried sage)**
- **½ cup dried cranberries**
- **2 cups chicken broth, divided**
- **½ pound turkey breast fillet**
- **¼ cup flour, divided**
- **½ cup apple juice**
- **2 teaspoons Dijon mustard**

On the Stove

1. In a big skillet over medium heat, heat 2 teaspoons oil. Add the onion and celery and season with salt and black pepper; cover and cook until softened, stirring occasionally.

2. Add the corn muffins and heat for 3 minutes, until lightly toasted. Stir in the sage, cranberries, and 1 cup broth and heat through.

3. Transfer to a bowl and cover with foil to keep warm. Wipe out the skillet.

4. Cut the turkey into serving-size pieces. Heat the remaining 2 teaspoons oil in the skillet and put 3 tablespoons flour in a shallow bowl. Season the turkey with salt and pepper, dredge with flour, and place in the hot oil.

5. Fry until golden brown on both sides, turning once; cover and cook until the internal temperature reaches 165°F. Transfer to a plate and cover with foil to keep warm.

6. Set the skillet over medium-high heat and add the apple juice, mustard, and the remaining 1 cup broth. Heat a few minutes, until slightly reduced, scraping up any browned bits with a whisk.

7. Put the remaining 1 tablespoon flour into a small mason jar with ¼ cup cold water; cover the jar and shake until smooth, then whisk into the sauce until slightly thickened.

8. Serve the sauce over the set-aside stuffing and turkey. Enjoy!

Dutch Oven Meatloaf

Ingredients

- 1 onion
- 4 pounds lean ground beef
- 2 cups breadcrumbs
- 3 eggs, lightly beaten
- 1 cup milk
- 1 cup ketchup, divided
- 2 teaspoons salt
- ½ teaspoon pepper
- Garlic powder, to taste
- Vegetable oil, as needed
- Baked or mashed potatoes, serving

Preparation

1. Finely chop onion and place in a large bowl.

2. Add ground beef, breadcrumbs, eggs, milk, ½ cup ketchup, salt, pepper, and garlic powder. Mix thoroughly.

In the Oven

1. Preheat oven to 350°F. Lightly grease bottom of Dutch oven with oil.

2. Spread prepared meatloaf mixture in pot; cover with lid. Place on lower rack in oven and cook for 50 to 60 minutes.

3. Uncover and spread remaining ½ cup ketchup over meatloaf.

4. Return to oven to bake uncovered for 15 minutes more or until fully cooked through (160°F internal temperature).

5. Let stand a few minutes before slicing. Serve with baked or mashed potatoes.

Over the Fire (24+ hot coals)

1. Lightly grease bottom of Dutch oven with vegetable oil. Spread prepared meatloaf mixture in pot and cover with lid.

2. Arrange about half of the hot coals in cooking ring underneath Dutch oven. Place remaining hot coals on lid. Cook about 40 minutes, rotating pot and lid several times during cooking and replenishing coals on top and bottom as needed to maintain temperature.

3. Transfer a few hot coals from bottom ring to lid and continue to cook about 20 minutes more. Carefully remove lid and spread remaining ½ cup ketchup over meatloaf; cover again and cook for 15 minutes more or until fully cooked through (160°F internal temperature).

4. Let stand a few minutes before slicing. Serve with baked or mashed potatoes.

Baked Garlic Shrimp

SERVES 2

Ingredients

- ¾ pound uncooked shrimp, peeled and deveined
- 1½ teaspoon minced garlic
- 1½ tablespoon dry white wine or chicken broth
- Sea salt and black pepper, to taste
- 2 tablespoons melted butter
- ¼ cup panko breadcrumbs
- 1 tablespoon fresh lemon juice
- Lemon zest, to garnish

In the Oven

10"

1. Preheat your oven to 425°F.

2. In a medium oven-safe skillet, combine the shrimp, garlic, and wine; toss to coat and spread out the shrimp in a single layer. Season with sea salt and black pepper.

3. Stir together the butter and breadcrumbs and sprinkle evenly over the shrimp. Bake for a quick 7 minutes or until the shrimp just begin to turn pink and opaque.

4. Preheat your broiler and broil the shrimp 2 to 3 minutes, until cooked through and the breadcrumbs are nicely toasted.

5. Remove the skillet from the broiler and drizzle the lemon juice over the shrimp. Then just sprinkle with lemon zest before serving for an extra hit of citrusy flavor.

6. Serve with Hasselbacks (see recipe on page 125).

Hasselbacks

SERVES 5

Ingredients

- **6 tablespoons butter, melted**
- **2 teaspoons minced garlic**
- **2 teaspoons dried parsley**
- **2 teaspoons dried rosemary**
- **5 Yukon gold potatoes**
- **Salt and black pepper, to taste**
- **Parmesan cheese**

In the Oven

1. Mix melted butter, minced garlic, and dried parsley and rosemary; brush a little in a kitchen-style Dutch oven.

2. Cut potatoes into crosswise slices, without cutting all the way through; set into the skillet. Brush some of the remaining butter between the slices; season with salt, black pepper, and Parmesan.

3. Bake at 425°F until tender, brushing often with remaining butter. Serve with Baked Garlic Shrimp (see recipe on page 124).

Shrimp Scampi with Zucchini Noodles

SERVES 4

Ingredients

- 1 zucchini
- 2 tablespoons unsalted butter
- 1½ tablespoons olive oil
- 1 tablespoon minced garlic
- ½ to ¾ pound large shrimp, peeled, deveined, and tails removed
- Salt and black pepper, to taste
- ¼ cup chicken broth
- Zest and juice from 1 lemon
- ⅛ teaspoon red pepper flakes
- Shredded Parmesan cheese, for topping
- Chopped tomatoes, for topping

On the Stove

10"

1. Cut the zucchini into long strands using a tool for cutting spiral vegetable noodles, then cut the strands to the desired length (or simply cut the zucchini into thin spaghetti-like pieces with a sharp knife). Set aside.

2. In a medium skillet, combine the butter and oil over medium-low heat until melted. Add the garlic and cook for 30 seconds.

3. Add the shrimp, salt, and black pepper and cook 5 minutes or until the shrimp turn pink and opaque, stirring often. Transfer to a plate.

4. Add the broth and lemon juice to the skillet, scraping up any browned bits. Add the set-aside zucchini noodles, lemon zest, and pepper flakes; stir in the set-aside shrimp.

5. Serve hot, topped with Parmesan and tomatoes.

Ingredients

- ¼ cup butter
- 1 onion, diced
- 8 ounces mushrooms, sliced
- 1 green bell pepper, diced
- 1 cup long-grain white rice, uncooked
- 1 teaspoon minced garlic
- 2 teaspoons Cajun seasoning
- 1 (10.75 ounce) can cream of mushroom soup
- 1 (10 ounce) can diced tomatoes with green chiles
- 2 cups vegetable broth
- 1 (12 ounce) package frozen cooked shrimp, deveined with tails on, thawed

SERVES 4

Louisiana Shrimp Pot

On the Stove

1. In the pot of a 10-inch kitchen-style Dutch oven over medium heat, melt ¼ cup butter; sauté the onion for 5 minutes.

2. Stir in the mushrooms, bell pepper, rice, garlic, seasoning, soup, tomatoes with green chiles, and broth. Bring to a boil and cover with the lid.

3. Simmer until the rice is tender, 15 to 20 minutes.

4. Add the shrimp, cover, and cook just until heated through. Serve alongside Swiss Crabmeat Bake (see recipe on page 130).

Over the Fire

1. Using a 10-inch camp-style Dutch oven instead, follow steps 1–2 above.

2. Simmer on a ring of hot coals with a few more on the lid.

3. Cook until the rice is tender, 15 to 20 minutes, rotating the pot and lid twice and stirring once.

4. Add the shrimp, cover, and cook just until heated through. Serve alongside Swiss Crabmeat Bake (see recipe on page 130).

Blackened Salmon with Mango Salsa

Ingredients

- 1 ripe mango, peeled, seeded, and chopped
- ¼ cup diced red bell pepper
- 2 tablespoons chopped red onion
- 1 tablespoon jalapeño pepper, finely diced
- 2 tablespoons fresh cilantro, chopped
- ½ teaspoon minced garlic
- 2 tablespoons lime juice
- Salt and black pepper, to taste
- 1½ teaspoons smoked paprika
- ¾ teaspoon dried oregano
- ¾ teaspoon dried thyme
- ¼ teaspoon cayenne pepper
- ¼ teaspoon white pepper
- ⅛ teaspoon onion powder
- ⅛ teaspoon garlic powder
- ¼ teaspoon sea salt
- ½ teaspoon sugar
- 2 (5 ounce) salmon fillets
- 2 tablespoons vegetable oil

Preparation

1. **For the salsa,** stir together the mango, bell pepper, onion, jalapeño, cilantro, garlic, lime juice, salt, and black pepper. Refrigerate until serving time.

2. Mix the paprika, oregano, thyme, cayenne, white pepper, onion powder, garlic powder, sea salt, and sugar and press seasoning mixture onto both sides of the salmon to adhere.

On the Stove

10"

1. Heat the oil in a skillet over medium-high heat and ever-so-carefully set the salmon into the hot oil.

2. Cover and fry a few minutes on each side, until cooked the way you like it. Serve with the chilled salsa.

Swiss Crabmeat Bake

Ingredients

- 1½ cup flour, divided
- 1 teaspoon salt, divided
- 2 teaspoons baking powder
- 1¼ cups shredded Swiss cheese, divided
- 2 tablespoons, plus ½ cup butter, divided
- ½ cup chopped green bell pepper
- ½ cup chopped onion
- 1 teaspoon dry mustard
- 1½ cups milk, divided
- 1 (8 ounce) package imitation crabmeat
- ½ cup Roma tomatoes, chopped
- 2 teaspoons Worcestershire sauce

Preparation

1. In a medium bowl, combine 1 cup flour, ½ teaspoon salt, and the baking powder.

2. Stir in ¼ cup Swiss cheese.

3. With a pastry blender or two knives, cut in 2 tablespoons butter until mixture is crumbly; reserve for later use.

On the Stove and in the Oven

1. Preheat oven to 400°F.

2. Meanwhile, place skillet on stovetop over medium heat and melt remaining ½ cup butter. Add bell pepper and onion; sauté until tender.

3. Gradually blend in remaining ½ cup flour, dry mustard, 1 cup milk, and remaining 1 cup cheese. Reduce heat to low and cook until cheese melts, stirring constantly.

4. Add crabmeat, tomatoes, and Worcestershire sauce; cook and stir until mixture is hot. Spread evenly in skillet and remove from heat.

5. To reserved flour mixture, add remaining ½ cup milk, and stir until dough forms. Drop dough by small spoonfuls over hot crab mixture, like a cobbler topping.

6. Transfer skillet to center rack in oven and bake uncovered about 25 minutes or until topping is golden brown and no longer doughy. Let cool slightly before serving alongside Louisiana Shrimp Pot (see recipe on page 128).

Over the Fire (24 hot coals)

1. Arrange about half of the hot coals in cooking ring underneath Dutch oven. Melt butter in pot.

2. Add bell pepper and onion; sauté until tender. Blend in remaining ½ cup flour, dry mustard, 1 cup milk and remaining 1 cup cheese.

3. Remove about 4 hot coals from cooking ring to reduce heat; cook mixture until cheese melts, stirring constantly. Add crabmeat, tomatoes, and Worcestershire sauce; cook and stir until mixture is hot.

4. Prepare dough and drop over hot crab mixture as directed above. Cover pot and place remaining hot coals on lid. Cook for 20 to 30 minutes or until topping is golden brown and no longer doughy.

5. Rotate pot and lid twice during cooking and adjust the number of coals on top and bottom as needed for even cooking. Let cool slightly before serving alongside Louisiana Shrimp Pot (see recipe on page 128).

SERVES
6

Ingredients

- 1 teaspoon black pepper
- 1 teaspoon cayenne pepper
- 1 teaspoon garlic powder
- 1 teaspoon onion powder
- 1 teaspoon paprika
- 1 teaspoon dried parsley
- 1 teaspoon salt
- ½ teaspoon dried oregano
- ½ teaspoon dried thyme
- 4 (4 ounce) catfish fillets, skinned
- ¾ cup butter, melted, divided

Blackened Cajun Catfish

SERVES 4

Preparation

In a small bowl, mix black pepper, cayenne pepper, garlic powder, onion powder, paprika, parsley, salt, oregano, and thyme. Press catfish fillets into spice mixture until well coated on all sides.

On the Stove

1. Place skillet on stovetop over high heat.
2. Pour about ¼ cup melted butter into skillet; set remaining ½ cup butter aside.
3. When butter in skillet is smoking hot, add catfish and cook until spices are burned onto fillets and fish is opaque and flaky inside, about 3 minutes on each side. Do not breathe smoke from burning spices.
4. Serve promptly, pouring reserved melted butter over catfish.

12"

Over the Fire (30 hot coals)

1. Place skillet on a grate over high heat (hot coals or gas grill) or set directly on a propane burner.
2. Pour about ¼ cup melted butter into skillet; set remaining ½ cup butter aside.
3. When butter in skillet is smoking hot, add catfish and cook until spices are burned onto fillets and fish is opaque and flaky inside, about 3 minutes on each side.
4. Adjust the number and placement of coals as needed to maintain heat. Do not breathe smoke from burning spices.
5. Serve promptly, pouring reserved melted butter over catfish.

12"

DESSERT

After all those hearty main dishes, make sure you leave some room for dessert. In this section, we have decadent sweets and treats for every appetite. It's the perfect way to end the day: by a fire with your loved ones, with cast-iron cooking making everything so much easier. You can worry about the dishes some other time. For now, it's time for dessert.

Peachy Raspberry Pie

Ingredients

- ⅓ cup flour
- ¼ cup brown sugar
- 1 teaspoon ground cinnamon
- ½ teaspoon ground ginger
- ¼ teaspoon ground nutmeg
- ½ teaspoon salt
- 4½ cups peeled, sliced fresh peaches (about 6)
- 2 tablespoons lemon juice

- 1 tablespoon vanilla
- ⅔ cup sugar, plus more for sprinkling
- 1 (14.1 ounce) package refrigerated pie crusts
- 1 cup fresh raspberries, mashed
- ¼ cup butter
- Whipped topping or ice cream, for serving

In the Oven

1. In a bowl, combine the flour, brown sugar, cinnamon, ginger, nutmeg, salt, peaches, lemon juice, vanilla, and ⅔ cup sugar. Press one crust over the bottom and up the sides of a 10-inch skillet.

2. Pour half the peach mixture into the pie shell and spoon the raspberries over the top. Spread with the remaining peach filling and dot with the butter.

3. Place the remaining crust over the filling, crimping edges together. Cut several slits in the top crust and sprinkle sugar evenly over the top.

4. Bake in a 350°F oven for an hour, until golden brown and bubbly. Shield edges with foil if necessary to prevent overbrowning.

5. Cool pie before slicing. Serve with whipped topping or ice cream if you'd like.

Over the Fire (26+ hot coals)

1. In a bowl, combine the flour, brown sugar, cinnamon, ginger, nutmeg, salt, peaches, lemon juice, vanilla, and ⅔ cup sugar. Press one crust into a 9-inch metal pie plate.

2. Follow steps 2–3 above.

3. Set the pie plate on risers (balls of foil or several canning jar rings work well) in the pot of a deep, 12-inch camp-style Dutch oven.

4. Cover and set on a ring of 9 hot coals with 17 hot coals on the lid. Bake 50 to 60 minutes, until golden brown and bubbly.

5. Rotate pot and lid several times and replenish coals as needed. Near the end of cooking time, add several hot coals to the center of the lid.

6. Cool pie before slicing. Serve with whipped topping or ice cream if you'd like.

SERVES
8

Pineapple Upside-Down Cake

SERVES 10

Ingredients

- 1 (20 ounce) can pineapple rings
- 1 (20 ounce) can crushed pineapple
- 1 (18.25 ounce) package yellow cake mix
- Eggs and oil, as directed on cake mix package
- ¼ cup butter
- 1½ cup brown sugar
- 1 teaspoon ground cinnamon
- ¼ cup sweetened flaked coconut, optional
- 10 maraschino cherries, drained

Preparation

1. Drain pineapple rings and crushed pineapple, reserving enough juice in a measuring cup to use in place of water listed on cake mix package (add water if short; discard any extra juice).

2. In a large mixing bowl, combine cake mix, eggs, oil, and pineapple juice; mix according to package instructions.

On the Stove and in the Oven

1. Preheat oven to 350°F.

2. Meanwhile, place skillet on stovetop over medium heat and melt butter.

3. Reduce heat and sprinkle brown sugar and cinnamon over butter, stirring to blend. Remove skillet from heat.

4. Arrange pineapple rings over brown sugar mixture. Spread crushed pineapple over rings, pressing down lightly with a spoon. Press coconut on top, if desired. Set a cherry in each pineapple ring. Pour prepared cake batter over pineapple layer.

5. Transfer skillet to center rack in oven and bake uncovered for 30 to 35 minutes or until cake is lightly browned and tests done with a toothpick.

6. Let cool in skillet for 5 to 10 minutes. Release edges of cake from skillet with a knife and carefully invert cake onto a platter.

7. Let cool completely before slicing and serving.

12"

Dutch Apple Crisp

SERVES 8-10

Ingredients

- **8 cups baking apples, peeled and thinly sliced (about 5 large)**
- **2 to 3 tablespoons lemon juice**
- **Ground cinnamon, to taste**
- **¾ cup sugar, divided**
- **¾ cup butter, cut into pieces, divided**
- **½ cup flour**
- **¼ cup brown sugar**
- **¼ teaspoon salt**
- **1 cup granola cereal**
- **Whipped topping or ice cream, for serving (optional)**

In the Oven

1. Line the pot of a 10-inch kitchen-style Dutch oven with foil and grease lightly. Dump in the apples.
2. Stir in the lemon juice, cinnamon, and ½ cup of the sugar; arrange evenly.
3. Scatter ¼ cup of the butter pieces over the apples.
4. In a bowl, stir together the flour, brown sugar, salt, granola, the remaining ¼ cup sugar, and more cinnamon and sprinkle evenly over the apple mixture. Scatter the remaining ½ cup butter over the top. Cover with the lid.
5. Bake in a 350°F oven for 45 minutes, until the apples are tender.
6. Serve warm or cold with or without whipped topping or ice cream.

Over the Fire

(18 hot coals)

10" with lid

1. Using a camp-style Dutch oven instead, follow steps 1–4 above.
2. Set the Dutch oven on a ring of 8 hot coals with 10 hot coals on the lid. Bake for 30 minutes or until the apples are tender.
3. Let the coals burn down and rotate the pot and lid every 8 to 10 minutes. Move a few coals to the center of the lid during the last few minutes of cooking.
4. Serve warm or cold with or without whipped topping or ice cream.

Granny's Apple Pie

Ingredients

- 1 (14.1 ounce) package refrigerated pie crust (2 count)
- 4 to 5 large apples (such as Granny Smith and/or Braeburn)
- ½ to ¾ cup sugar
- 2 tablespoons brown sugar
- 1 teaspoon ground cinnamon
- ⅛ teaspoon ground nutmeg
- 2 tablespoons flour
- 2 tablespoons butter, cut into pieces
- Egg white, optional
- Coarse sugar, optional
- Ice cream, optional
- Caramel ice cream topping, optional

Preparation

1. Allow wrapped pie crusts to stand at room temperature for 15 minutes to soften.

2. Peel and core apples; slice evenly.

3. In a large bowl, mix sugar, brown sugar, cinnamon, nutmeg, and flour; add apples and toss until coated.

In the Oven

1. Preheat oven to 350°F.

2. Unroll one pie crust and press over bottom and up sides of skillet. Spread prepared apple mixture over crust. Dot with pieces of butter.

3. Unroll remaining pie crust and place over apples, crimping crust edges together. If desired, whisk egg white until frothy and brush over pie crust; sprinkle with coarse sugar.

4. Cut several slits in top crust to vent steam. Place skillet on center rack in oven (with baking sheet underneath) and bake uncovered about 1 hour or until golden brown and bubbly. Shield edges with aluminum foil if necessary to prevent excess browning.

5. Cool for 30 minutes before slicing. Serve pie wedges with ice cream and caramel topping, if desired.

Over the Fire (23+ hot coals)

1. Unroll one pie crust and press over bottom and up sides of a 9-inch-deep metal pie plate, allowing excess crust to hang over rim.

2. Spread prepared apple mixture over crust. Dot with pieces of butter. Unroll remaining pie crust and place over apples. Overlap crust edges and crimp to seal.

3. If desired, whisk egg white until frothy and brush over pie crust; sprinkle with coarse sugar. Cut several slits in top crust to vent steam.

4. Prepare riser in Dutch oven. Set pie plate on riser and cover pot with lid.

5. Arrange about one-third of the hot coals in cooking ring under Dutch oven. Place remaining hot coals on lid. Cook for 50 to 60 minutes or until golden brown and bubbly.

6. Rotate pot and lid several times during cooking and replenish coals on top and bottom as needed to maintain cooking temperature. To promote browning on top, add several hot coals near handle on lid toward end of cooking time.

7. Cool for 30 minutes before slicing. Serve pie wedges with ice cream and caramel topping, if desired.

10" with lid

Ingredients

- **1 pint fresh blueberries**
- **1 (21 ounce) can blueberry pie filling**
- **Zest and juice of 1 lemon**
- **2 (12.4 ounce) tubes refrigerated cinnamon rolls with frosting**

Cinnamon Rolls with Blueberries

SERVES 16

On the Stove and in the Oven

12"

1. In the pot of a greased 12-inch kitchen-style Dutch oven, combine blueberries, pie filling, zest, and juice.
2. Cook on the stovetop until bubbly, stirring often.
3. Separate the rolls and arrange over the blueberry mixture; set the frosting aside.
4. Bake in a 350°F oven for 20 minutes, until golden brown and cooked through. Scoop rolls and blueberry mixture onto serving plates and spread the set-aside frosting on the rolls.

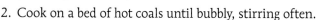

Over the Fire (24 hot coals)

12" with lid

1. In the pot of a greased 12-inch camp-style Dutch oven, combine blueberries, pie filling, zest, and juice.
2. Cook on a bed of hot coals until bubbly, stirring often.
3. Separate the rolls and arrange over the blueberry mixture; set the frosting aside. Cover the pot and set on a ring of 12 fresh hot coals, with 12 fresh hot coals spread out on the lid.
4. Cook for 10 minutes, rotate the pot and lid, remove 5 coals from underneath and replenish the top coals for even cooking.
5. Cook 10 minutes longer, until the rolls are golden brown and cooked through, checking a few times during cooking. Scoop rolls and blueberry mixture onto serving plates and spread the set-aside frosting on the rolls.

Cherry-Cream Roll-Ups

SERVES 12

Ingredients

- ½ cup brown sugar
- ¼ teaspoon ground nutmeg
- 2 teaspoons ground cinnamon
- 12 slices sandwich bread, crusts removed
- ¾ cup cream cheese, softened
- ¾ cup cherry pie filling (about half of a 21-ounce can)
- ¼ cup sliced almonds
- 2 tablespoons butter
- 2 eggs
- 3 tablespoons milk

On the Stove

12"

1. In a shallow bowl, mix the brown sugar, nutmeg, and cinnamon; set aside.

2. Flatten the bread slices and smear each with 1 tablespoon cream cheese and the pie filling; sprinkle with almonds and roll up tightly.

3. Melt the butter in a big skillet.

4. In a shallow bowl, whisk together the eggs and milk; coat the roll-ups in the mixture and set seam side down in the melted butter.

5. Cook until golden brown, turning as needed.

6. Coat hot roll-ups in the set-aside brown sugar mixture. Serve warm.

Over the Fire

12"

Using a grate over a campfire instead, follow all steps above.

Dutch Oven Cinnamon-Pecan Cake

Ingredients

- 2 ¼ cups flour
- ½ teaspoon salt
- 1 tablespoon, plus ½ teaspoon ground cinnamon, divided
- 1 cup sugar, divided
- 1 cup brown sugar
- 1 teaspoon baking powder
- 1 cup milk
- ½ cup vegetable oil
- 1 egg, beaten
- ½ cup chopped pecans
- Whipped topping or vanilla or cinnamon ice cream, for serving

Preparation

1. In a medium bowl, stir together flour, salt, 1 tablespoon cinnamon, ¾ cup sugar, brown sugar, and baking powder.

2. In a large measuring cup, whisk together milk, oil, and egg. Add milk mixture to dry ingredients and stir until batter is smooth.

3. In a small bowl, mix remaining ½ teaspoon cinnamon, remaining ¼ cup sugar, and pecans; reserve topping for later use.

In the Oven

1. Preheat oven to 350°F. Line bottom of Dutch oven with a circle of parchment paper. Lightly grease paper and sides of pot with nonstick cooking spray.

2. Spread batter evenly in pot. Sprinkle reserved topping mixture over top, swirling into batter lightly with a knife, if desired.

3. Bake for 35 to 40 minutes or until cake tests done with a toothpick.

4. Let cool slightly before slicing. Serve warm or at room temperature with a dollop of whipped topping or scoop of ice cream.

Over the Fire (22 hot coals)

1. Line bottom of Dutch oven with a circle of parchment paper. Lightly grease paper and sides of pot with nonstick cooking spray.

2. Spread batter evenly in pot. Sprinkle reserved topping mixture over top, swirling into batter lightly with a knife, if desired. Cover Dutch oven with lid.

3. Arrange about one-third of the hot coals in cooking ring underneath Dutch oven. Place remaining hot coals on lid. Cook for 30 to 40 minutes or cake tests done with a toothpick.

4. Rotate pot and lid twice during cooking and adjust the number of coals on top and bottom as needed for even cooking.

5. Let cool slightly before slicing. Serve warm or at room temperature with a dollop of whipped topping or scoop of ice cream.

Ingredients

- **1 cup butter, softened**
- **1 cup sugar**
- **2 eggs**
- **2 teaspoons vanilla**
- **1½ cups flour**
- **½ teaspoon salt**
- **2 teaspoons baking powder**
- **1½ cups graham cracker crumbs**
- **1 (9.3 ounce) package chocolate bars (6 count)**
- **2 (7 ounce) jars marshmallow crème**

S'mores Bars

In the Oven

1. Line the pot of a 12-inch skillet with parchment paper.

2. In a big bowl, mix the butter, sugar, and eggs until light and creamy. Stir in the vanilla, flour, salt, baking powder, and crumbs.

3. Spread two-thirds of the dough evenly into the skillet. Arrange the chocolate bars over the dough, breaking as needed, and cover with spoonfuls of marshmallow crème. Scoop the remaining dough over the top.

4. Bake in a 325°F oven for 45 minutes or until the marshmallow layer begins to brown and the dough is cooked through.

5. Let stand a few minutes, then remove by lifting the parchment paper.

Over the Fire (24 hot coals)

1. Using a 12-inch camp-style Dutch oven instead, follow steps 1–3 above.

2. Cover the pot with the lid and set on a ring of 8 hot coals with 16 hot coals on the lid.

3. Bake 25 to 35 minutes, until golden brown and cooked through.

4. Rotate pot and lid every 10 minutes, checking frequently and adjusting coals as needed. Let coals burn down without replenishing.

5. When marshmallow layer starts to brown, remove 4 coals from the lid and move several of the remaining coals toward the center of the lid.

6. Let stand a few minutes, then remove by lifting the parchment paper.

Fudgy Chocolate Cake

SERVES 15

Ingredients

- **1 (3.9 ounce) package chocolate instant pudding mix**
- **1½ cups milk**
- **1 (18.25 ounce) package chocolate cake mix**
- **1½ cups semisweet chocolate chips**

In the Oven

12" with lid

1. Line the pot of a 12-inch kitchen-style Dutch oven with parchment paper.

2. In a bowl, whisk together the pudding mix and milk until thickened. Stir in the cake mix until well combined (batter will be thick).

3. Spread evenly in the pot and sprinkle with chocolate chips. Cover with the lid.

4. Bake in a 350°F oven for 30 to 40 minutes, until the cake tests done with a toothpick and the edges pull away from the sides.

5. Remove cake from the pot by lifting the parchment paper. Slice and serve.

Over the Fire

(26 hot coals)

12" with lid

1. Using a camp-style Dutch oven instead, follow steps 1–3 above.

2. Set the Dutch oven on a ring of 9 hot coals with 17 hot coals on the lid. Bake 30 to 40 minutes or until the cake tests done with a toothpick and the edges pull away from the sides.

3. Rotate the pot and lid and check for doneness several times during cooking. Let coals burn down before replenishing a few.

4. Remove cake from the pot by lifting the parchment paper. Slice and serve.

Nutty Hot Fudge Cake

SERVES 10

Ingredients

- 1¼ cups sugar, divided
- 5 tablespoons unsweetened cocoa powder, divided
- ½ cup brown sugar
- 1 cup flour
- 2 teaspoons baking powder
- ¼ teaspoon salt
- ½ cup milk
- 1 teaspoon vanilla extract
- 2 tablespoons butter, melted
- ¾ cup chopped pecans
- Ice cream, for serving

Preparation

1. In a small bowl, mix ½ cup sugar, 2 tablespoons cocoa powder, and brown sugar; set topping aside.

2. In a medium bowl, stir together flour, remaining ¾ cup sugar, baking powder, salt, and remaining 3 tablespoons cocoa powder.

3. Add milk and vanilla; stir until blended. Stir in melted butter and pecans.

In the Oven

10"

1. Preheat oven to 350°F. Grease bottom of Dutch oven with nonstick cooking spray.

2. Line pot with a circle of parchment paper, extending paper 2 inches up sides; spray paper.

3. Spread batter in Dutch oven. Sprinkle set-aside topping over batter. Pour 1 cup boiling water over top of cake, but do not stir.

4. Place Dutch oven on center rack in oven and bake uncovered for 30 to 35 minutes, or until cake tests done with a toothpick.

5. Remove from oven and let stand 5 to 10 minutes. Carefully invert cake onto a lightly greased platter. Remove parchment paper and cool at least 15 minutes before cutting.

6. Serve with ice cream if you'd like.

Over the Fire (About 22 hot coals)

1. Prepare Dutch oven with nonstick cooking spray and parchment paper as directed above.

2. Spread batter in Dutch oven. Sprinkle set-aside topping over batter. Pour 1 cup boiling water over top of cake but do not stir. Cover Dutch oven.

3. Arrange about one-third of the hot coals in cooking ring underneath Dutch oven. Place remaining hot coals on lid.

4. Cook for 25 to 35 minutes or until cake tests done with a toothpick. Rotate pot and lid twice during cooking and adjust the number of coals on top and bottom as needed for even cooking.

5. Remove Dutch oven from heat and let stand about 5 minutes. Carefully invert cake onto a lightly greased platter. Remove parchment paper and cool at least 15 minutes before cutting.

6. Serve with ice cream if you'd like.

Jumbo Chipper Cookie

SERVES 16

Ingredients

- 2¼ cups flour
- 1 teaspoon baking soda
- ½ teaspoon salt
- ½ cup vegetable shortening
- ½ cup butter, softened
- ¾ cup sugar
- ¾ cup brown sugar
- 2 teaspoons vanilla extract
- 2 eggs
- 1 cup semi-sweet chocolate chips
- 1 cup butterscotch chips
- Ice cream, for serving

Preparation

1. In a medium bowl, whisk together flour, baking soda, and salt.

2. In a large mixing bowl, beat shortening and butter until creamy. Beat in sugar, brown sugar, and vanilla. Add eggs and beat well.

3. Gradually beat in dry ingredients until blended. Stir in chocolate and butterscotch chips.

In the Oven

12"

1. Preheat oven to 350°F. Lightly grease skillet with nonstick cooking spray.

2. Press prepared cookie dough evenly in bottom of skillet, flattening lightly. Bake about 30 minutes or until edges pull away from side of pan and top is golden brown.

3. Remove from oven to a cooling rack and let cool in skillet for 15 minutes before removing from skillet or cutting into wedges.

4. Serve wedges alone or with ice cream.

Over the Fire

(About 26 hot coals)

12" with lid

1. Lightly grease Dutch oven with nonstick cooking spray.

2. Press prepared cookie dough evenly in bottom of pot, flattening lightly. Cover pot with lid.

3. Arrange about ⅓ hot coals in cooking ring underneath Dutch oven. Place remaining hot coals on lid. Cook for 25 to 35 minutes or until edges pull away from side of pot and top is golden brown.

4. Rotate pot and lid several times during cooking and adjust the number of coals on top and bottom as needed for even browning.

5. Uncover and let cool in Dutch oven for 15 minutes before removing from pot or cutting into wedges.

6. Serve wedges alone or with ice cream.

TIP
Similar cookie recipes may be used following these cooking methods.

Index